Microsoft® Word
for
Terrified Teachers

Editor:
Kathy Humrichouse

Editorial Project Manager:
Elizabeth Morris, Ph.D.

Editor in Chief:
Sharon Coan, M.S. Ed.

Creative Director:
Elayne Roberts

Product Manager:
Phil Garcia

Imaging:
Alfred Lau

Acknowledgements:
Microsoft® Word software is ©1991–1998 Microsoft Corporation. All Rights Reserved. *Microsoft® Word* is a trademark of Microsoft Corporation, registered in the U.S. and other countries. Microsoft® Clip art ©1997 All rights reserved.

Publishers:
Rachelle Cracchiolo, M.S. Ed.
Mary Dupuy Smith, M.S. Ed.

Authors:

Paula Patton and Karla Neeley Hase

Teacher Created Materials, Inc.
6421 Industry Way
Westminster, CA 92683
www.teachercreated.com
ISBN-1-57690-438-5
©1999 Teacher Created Materials, Inc.
Made in U.S.A.

Table of Contents

Table of Contents *(cont.)*

Table of Contents *(cont.)*

Table of Contents *(cont.)*

Introduction

At the end of each school year, you look at all of the work you have done preparing lessons, planning special events, and keeping track of all of those students. It was an awesome task to say the least. Classes are over and the kids are sent home, but you are still challenged with the desire to do it better next year. How are you going to top this year? You dream of ways to lighten the load while accomplishing more and more.

You decide to add to your toolbox and to let the computer become your personal assistant, an ever present, supportive, classroom aide. The computer is a toolbox, and the programs are your tools. *Microsoft Word* is no different than the Egyptians' use of ramps assisting them in their monumental building projects. *Microsoft Word* becomes your simple machine to use to complete many burdensome tasks.

Microsoft Word can be used not only to build curriculum and classroom presentations but also to make invitations, certificates, newsletters, and much more. Your students can work with you to create a homepage for the Internet so that people from around the world can learn about your class and their activities. The computer and *Microsoft Word* can provide a window to the world for both you and your students.

As you work through this book, remember to have fun. Be creative. *Microsoft Word* is your brush, while the computer is your canvas. Enjoy!

Which Version?

It is important to note that this book was written with reference to the features in *Microsoft Word 97* for Windows® and *Microsoft Word 98* for Macintosh®. Many of the same tools, features, and instructions apply to previous versions of *Word* (*Word 95* for Windows and *Word 6.0* for Macintosh) with only slight variations. The examples and templates on the accompanying CD-ROM can be opened using either version 95 or 97 on the Windows platform, and either *Word 6.0* or *Word 98* on the Macintosh platform.

What Can Microsoft Word Do for Me?

Microsoft Word is a word processing program. At its simplest, it turns your computer into a typewriter. You can write notes or turn out professional-looking documents. You can publish pages on the Internet or create newsletters, term papers, and lesson plans. Are you terrified yet? Are you saying, "Maybe you can, after years of studying, but I'm a classroom teacher"? "I don't have time to read all those thick manuals." Forget it. You do not have time for needless worry, either. *Microsoft Word* is very powerful, true, but it is also the easiest word processing program I have ever used. And, by the way, I am a classroom teacher, too.

Microsoft Word has Wizards to help you with many of the tasks you want to do. A Wizard asks you a few questions about what you want to say and then puts it into a great-looking document for you. There is a letter wizard so that you can concentrate on what you want to say instead of trying to remember how to do block style. There is a résumé wizard that turns out résumés you can be proud of in a matter of minutes. Want to do mailing labels? There is a wizard for that, too. Need to produce envelopes, memos, faxes, and newsletters? *Microsoft Word* provides a wizard for all of these. Even if your principal comes in and says, "Podunk Elementary has a page on the Web, and I think we should too." No need to worry. *Microsoft Word* has a wizard for that, also.

You can easily make templates for the tasks you do often—for instance, lesson plans, letters to parents, etc. A template is a pattern you can create and then replace only the parts that change. It can save a lot of time, and I have never seen a teacher that does not need to save time. You can even use a feature called "mail merge" that will personalize parent letters for you.

Microsoft Word has a spell and grammar checker that works as you type, so that you can make your corrections as you go. If that disturbs your concentration, it can be turned off, and you can check your spelling when you are ready. There is a built-in thesaurus for those of us frequently at a loss for words.

You can add tables, drawings, or pictures to any document. Three-dimensional effects really add pizzazz to your presentations, and full compatibility with other *Microsoft Office* products means you can include data from other applications into your documents. The ability to import Johnny's grades from your spreadsheet program into a notice of concern to his parents can be very helpful. Including the addresses and telephone numbers of all of the room parents in a letter about the End-of-School party (without having to type them into the letter), can save time and effort. A teacher's presentation to the school board about her students' participation in the "Great American Mail Race" can be quite impressive with fancy Word Art and illustrations. Using *Microsoft Word* can save you time and can allow you to do things for yourself you once would have had to depend on (and pay) a printer to do for you. It allows you to create documents that impress friends, relatives, co-workers, students, administrators, and school boards!

Using This Book

Microsoft Word for Terrified Teachers is written so that it can be used as a tutorial and later as a reference manual. Each section introduces a concept, tells how to accomplish a task, and gives you the opportunity to practice your newly learned skill. A glossary and index are included at the end of the book and can be used as yet another tool in your toolbox.

Tips for Success are presented in each section to share with you those little "nice-to-know" pieces of information that can save you hours of stress and headache. The tips are easy to spot throughout the book. Just look for the star in the left margin.

Try This is designed to let you experiment with new skills while learning each concept. After successfully practicing the skill, you can check it as a task well done and move forward to that section's activity.

The activities allow you the opportunity to practice the skill further. As you work through each activity, you will discover techniques that will help you use *Microsoft Word* more efficiently in future projects. Use this chart to assist you when following the directions for projects and activities.

Instruction	What To Do
BOLD CAPITALS	Select this pulldown menu from the Menu Bar.
Bold Italics	Make this selection from the pulldown menu.
Bold	Choose this button, tool, or key.
(filename)	Type this word or sentence, or this is the name of a file.

The last section of this book contains several large projects where you will combine the skills learned throughout the book. Do not be surprised if you find that some of these ideas can be used as the basis for your own classroom projects.

Starting Microsoft Word

Let's get on with the program. Rather, let's get into the program. Using *Windows 95*, *Windows 98*, and *Windows NT*, you can start *Microsoft Word* in two ways. First of all, if your computer is set to launch the *Microsoft Office* Shortcut Bar each time you turn it on, you can start *Microsoft Word* by clicking the **New Office Document** button on the toolbar.

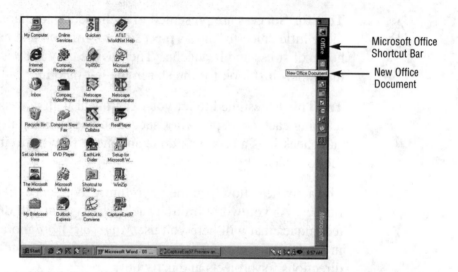

Microsoft Office Shortcut Bar

New Office Document

Then select a new **Blank Document** from the **New Office Document** box.

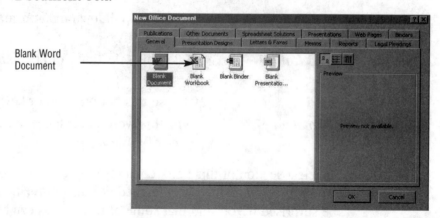

Blank Word Document

Another way to start *Microsoft Word* is by using the **Start** button. Click the **Start** button at the bottom of your screen. Select **Programs** from the menu that appears. Scroll to *Microsoft Word* and click.

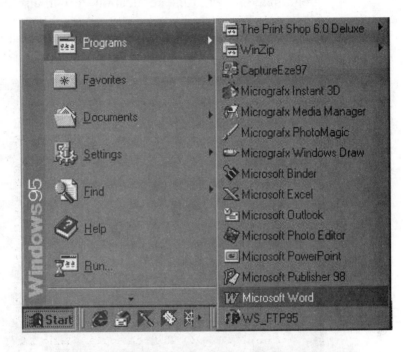

Now *Microsoft Word* is ready to go!

If you are using the Macintosh version of *Microsoft Office 98*, double-click the *Microsoft Office 98* folder that is located on your hard drive. This will open the folder, and a list of all of the files will be visible. Double-click the *Microsoft Word* application program icon to start the application. It will also open to a new, blank document.

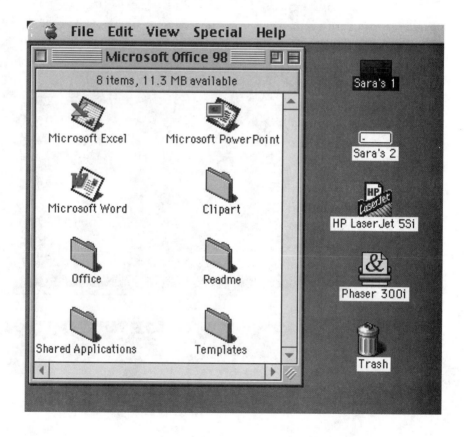

What Is All of This Stuff?

OK, you have gotten into *Microsoft Word*. There is a blank screen with all sorts of scary stuff surrounding it. How are you ever going to memorize what all of these little symbols mean, much less how to use them? Simple, you probably will not. You will learn to use the things you need to use, as the need arises. That is what reference books are for. When you need to track changes in a document, you will grab your *Microsoft Word* reference book, ask the Office Assistant, or click the **HELP** menu. Until then, you may be perfectly happy never knowing how the little grayed-out **TRK** button on the status bar is used. However, here is a list of some of the things about which you might be curious.

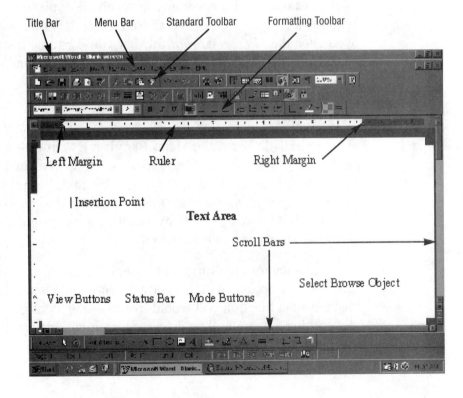

Title Bar (Windows Only):

In Windows, the Title Bar is the colored bar at the top of the screen that tells you what program you are running (*Microsoft Word*). Each window has its own title bar. After you save the document you are working on, its name will appear on the title bar of that document window. The title bar also has the **Minimize** (a minus) button, the **Maximize/Restore** button, and the **Close** (an X) button.

If you minimize a document window, it disappears from the screen and reappears as a little rectangle on the taskbar. You can get it back at any time by clicking the rectangle on the taskbar. Clicking the **Maximize/Restore** button changes the size of the document or program window. Try it now. It is useful for seeing everything you have open and for working in several documents simultaneously. Clicking the **Close** button closes the window. If you click the *Microsoft Word* title bar **Close** button, it will close the entire *Microsoft Word* program. The **Close** button on a document window will close only that document.

Menu Bar:

Under the Title Bar is the Menu Bar. It is a strip with words, and each word, when selected, reveals a menu. In Windows, you can use the keyboard instead of the mouse by holding down the **Alt** key while you press the letter that is underlined in the menu. You can also hold down the **Alt** key and then use the right and left arrows to move through the menu.

With a Macintosh platform, click the menu title you want to use and a list of options will drop down. Pull your cursor through the list until the function you would like to use is highlighted and then let go. Each menu will be discussed later, but you can just explore them now.

Pull down the **TOOLS** menu now. In the **TOOLS** menu, you will see three little dots after the *Spelling and Grammar*, *Word Count* and *AutoSummarize* items, as well as after several other options on the menu. These little dots, which are known as an ellipsis, tell you that if you click this item, a dialog box will appear. These dialog boxes will give you options or let you enter information before continuing with their job.

Tools	Table	Window	Work	Help
Spelling and Grammar... ⌘⌥L				
Language ▶				
Word Count...				
AutoSummarize...				
AutoCorrect...				
Track Changes ▶				
Merge Documents...				
Protect Document...				
Mail Merge...				
Envelopes and Labels...				
Letter Wizard...				
Macro ▶				
Templates and Add-Ins...				
Customize...				
Preferences...				

Now look at the *Language*, *Track Changes*, and *Macro* items. You will see little side-pointing triangles to the far right of these items. These triangles tell you that stopping on this item will open submenus with more options.

Sometimes there will be a keystroke shortcut listed next to a menu item, such as *Spelling and Grammar* on the **TOOLS** menu. This means that you can press **F7** (Windows) or the **Command** (⌘), **Option**, and **L** keys (Macintosh) to check your spelling and grammar at any time without going to the menu bar. Knowing some of these keystroke shortcuts will save you time.

If a menu item is grayed out, it is unavailable to you at the moment. For example, if you look at the **TABLE** menu now, most of the items are probably grayed out, because you do not have a table in your document. If you choose **Insert Table** and add a table to your document, then the other choices will be available to you.

Some menu items can be turned off and on. Pull down the **View** menu and show the submenu *Toolbars*. Notice that there are checkmarks in front of some of the items in the submenu. These checkmarks indicate that the *Standard*, *Formatting*, and *Drawing* toolbars are active now. If you click one of these, the toolbar will disappear from your screen. If you select the **Picture** menu item, for example, the **Picture** toolbar will appear on your screen and a checkmark will be placed in front of the menu item *Picture* in this submenu to indicate that this toolbar is active.

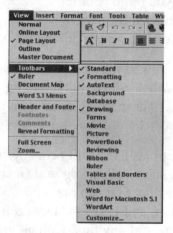

Standard Toolbar:

The **Standard** toolbar, which most of the time is directly under the Menu Bar, has buttons for several of the common functions. Creating a new document, opening an existing document, saving, printing, previewing your document, checking your spelling, copying, and pasting are a few of these functions. You can do each of these using the menu bars, but most of the time using the **Standard** toolbar is faster. If you forget what an icon represents, just put your cursor on the icon, leave it for a second or two, and *Microsoft Word* will tell you what that icon represents.

Formatting Toolbar:

The **Formatting** toolbar, like the **Standard** toolbar, is a default toolbar. That is, unless you choose to change it, it will always be at the top of your screen, under the **Standard** toolbar. This toolbar saves a great deal of time and frustration by allowing you to change your formatting with a click of the mouse button. You can change the font, or style of lettering, and the font size. You can make your printing **bold**, *italic,* or <u>underlined</u>. You can easily align your text left, right, or center. You can change the color of your printing or highlight certain important passages. Each of these icons, like the ones on the **Standard** toolbar, will tell you its function when you pause briefly on it with your cursor.

Office Shortcut Bar (Windows Only):

The Office Shortcut Bar (Windows), which appears on your desktop and also on the screen when you are in *Microsoft Word*, lets you switch back and forth between components of *Microsoft Office* easily, open new documents, make notes to yourself, and several other options. If you are not into all of the *Microsoft Office* components or it is something you just do not want to deal with having on your screen right now, you can easily remove it. Just click the little four-colored square at the far right of the bar or at the top if the bar appears on the side of your screen, then choose **Exit**. You will have the choice of banishing it forever or just until you restart your computer the next time.

The Office Manager (Macintosh) is the four-colored square icon which appears on your menu bar next to the application or finder icon. By selecting this icon, you can move between the different *Microsoft* applications that are installed on your computer. To customize the look of Office Manager to fit your needs, select the **Customize** option. A dialog box will open to allow you to choose the applications that will reside in the drop down menu.

Ruler:

When you are working in an actual document, a ruler shows the left and right margins along with your tab and indentations. To change these settings, simply place your cursor on them, then click and drag.

Insertion Point:

The Insertion Point is the little blinking line that shows where the next word you are going to type will appear.

View Buttons:

The View buttons are the four tiny little buttons located at the far left of the bottom scroll bar at the lower edge of your document screen. You may find it simpler to use the **VIEW** menu on your menu bar because it is difficult to remember which button is which. You may, however, find these buttons very useful. *Microsoft Word* allows you to do nearly everything in several different ways.

The first button on the left is the **Normal View** and is the default view. Most of your typing, editing, and formatting will probably be done in 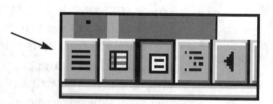 this view. It shows page breaks, your font style and size, and most formatting. It does not show headers, footers, or frames. Because it does not show all formatting, it is the fastest way to scroll through a document.

The second button is the **Online Layout** view. This button was not available in *Microsoft Office* for *Windows 95*. This view makes it easier to read a document because the text is larger and each page fits entirely on the screen, and you do not have to use the scroll. It also has a document map on the side that is useful if you are working on a large document, but you must always keep in mind that it will not look this way when it is printed.

The third button is the **Page Layout** view. In this view, the document looks exactly the way it will look when it is printed. You can see your headers and footers, page numbers, graphics and frames, and all of the other formatting you put in to make your document professional. Most people switch back and forth between this view and Normal.

The last View Button is the **Outline** view. This view allows you to make outlines easily. Your lesson plans will look professional, and you will not have to bother with tabs or decide which letter or number to use. There are several other ways to use this view which will be discussed later.

Status Bar:

The Status Bar shows you the number of the page on which your insertion point is located. This will not always be the same as the page you are currently viewing on your computer screen. For example, you scroll up to make sure that you have included an item on a previous page, but then found that you did not. If you start to type in the information without moving your insertion point to that page, your inserted information will appear wherever your little blinking line is located.

The next item on the Status Bar is Section. You change sections in your document by going to **INSERT** on the menu bar and choosing the type of break you want performed at the insertion point. After the Section you will see a fraction. This fraction tells you how many total pages you have in your document, and which one of those pages you are viewing. For example, if the fraction is 8/24, the page on your screen is page 8 of a 24 page document.

The next item on the Status Bar tells you where your insertion point is on the page. The measurement is in inches and measures from the top edge of the page. This will be helpful if you are trying to decide whether or not to insert a particular graphic at a specific point.

The next item tells you the line number where your insertion point is active. The next item denotes the column, which is the distance, in characters, from the left margin to your insertion point.

You now come to several grayed out buttons. By double-clicking any one of these buttons, you will cause the mode to change. The **OVR** button toggles between Insert, which moves characters that are to the right of the insertion point to the right as you type, and Overtype, which types over the existing characters, wiping them out. **REC** stands for Record Macro, **TRK** allows you to track changes, and **EXT** allows you to Extend Selection. A greater explanation of these buttons can be found in the help menu.

The last item that you can see on the Status Bar is the **Spelling and Grammar Status** button. If *Microsoft Word* is checking the spelling and grammar, a pencil appears to be writing in the little book. If there are errors, an X appears on the book. If the errors have been corrected (or ignored) a check appears on the book.

Scroll Bars:

You can use the two scroll bars to move the document up and down or from side to side on the screen. Click the black triangle at the top of the vertical scroll bar to move up one line, or click the black triangle at the bottom to move down one line. Hold the arrow down to continue moving. You can click and drag the scroll box to move quickly through the document (the scroll box will show your approximate location in the document). By clicking in the area just below the up triangle, you will move up one screen. If you click in the area just above the down triangle, you will move down one screen. If you hold down the mouse button in this area you will move very quickly, a page at a time, through the document. The horizontal bar works in the same way as the vertical bar, moving right and left instead of up and down.

When you first open *Microsoft Word*, the double "up" triangle at the bottom of the vertical scroll bar will take you to the previous page. The double "down" triangle will take you to the next page. If you click the small circle between these two double triangles, called the **Browse by Object** button, *Microsoft Word* will allow you to choose what function the double triangles will do. Click this button and allow your mouse pointer to linger on each choice to see what you can do with this option. Again, using these arrows to browse does not change your insertion point. You must move the I-beam and click the mouse to do that.

Office Assistant:

The Office Assistant is a cute little guy who offers help when you need it and tries to answer your questions. When you first start *Microsoft Word*, he appears in a little box to welcome you to *Microsoft Word* and to offer his help. In Windows, the default assistant is a paperclip with personality named Clippit. You can click the Assistant, type your question, and click **Search**. Suggestions as to which help file you need are presented within a dialog box.

With a Macintosh platform, the default assistant is a computer monitor named Max. To activate the Office Assistant at any time, click the dialog bubble with a question mark located on your Standard toolbar. Type in your question and click **Search**.

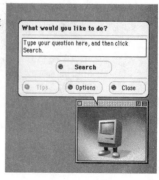

Sometimes you do not even have to ask for help. When you start to do a different function, the Assistant will just appear and ask you if you need help. At various times when you are inactive or waiting for the printer to start, the little guy will do some interesting and amusing antics, not unlike your students. However, he has one feature that students do not have. You can turn him off if you are in a hurry or he just begins to bug you.

You can also change Assistants if you would like. Click the Office Assistant or the **Office Assistant** button on the **Standard** toolbar and choose **Options**. In the **Gallery** tab, you are able to scroll through the different Assistants available to you. Also, if you have access to the Internet, there are some additional Assistants available to download from the *Microsoft Office* Web site.

Hoverbot

The Genius

Will

Power Pup

Office Logo

Scribble

Mother Nature

The Dot

Changing the Way the Screen Looks

Microsoft Word provides you with several options for customizing how your screen will appear from the **VIEW** pulldown menu on your menu bar.

The **Zoom** option allows you to adjust the size of type on the screen to your own personal preference. The increased size option also aids in proofreading complicated materials including numerical data. The **Whole Page** option lets you view the complete page and adjust margins, page breaks, and other formatting to enhance the appearance of your document.

Try This:

- Click **VIEW** from the menu bar.
- Select **Zoom**.

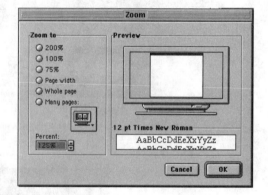

- You can also access the **Zoom** option from your toolbar.

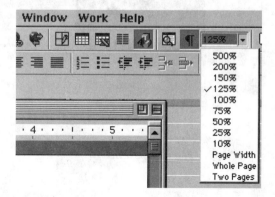

Layouts for your document include **Normal**, **Outline Layout**, and **Page Layout**. Each of these options will change the appearance of your document on the screen. Here is an example of each using this document.

Normal

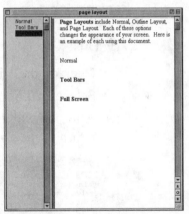

Outline Layout

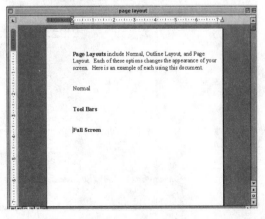

Page Layout

Toolbars can be moved and rearranged. You may chose to have only those toolbars showing that you use on a regular basis. Toolbars can be selected and deselected.

Try This:

- Select **VIEW** from the menu bar.
- Choose *Toolbars* and another drop down menu will appear.
- Select or deselect toolbars by clicking the name of the desired toolbar.

The **Full Screen** option removes everything from your screen except the document you are working on and the **Close Full Screen** box.

Try This:

- Click on the **VIEW** option from the menu bar.
- Select *Full Screen*.
- After viewing the full screen, click **Close Full Screen** to return to the Page Layout.

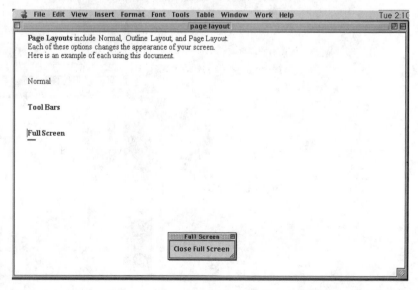

What are those Funny Little Dots and Symbols?

How do I get rid of them? When you see paragraph symbols at the ends of paragraphs and on blank lines and dots between every word, the **Show/Hide** button is activated on your toolbar. The paragraph symbol looks like a backwards upper case P. The space symbol looks like a dot.

Paragraph symbol

Space Dots

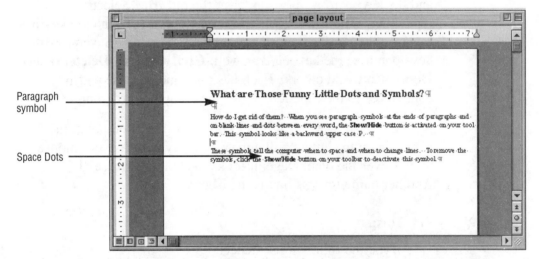

These symbols tell the computer when to space and when to change lines. To remove the paragraph and space dot symbols, click the **Show/Hide** button on your toolbar to deactivate this feature.

Entering Text

Whether you call it keyboarding, data entry, text entry, or just plain old typing, getting your ideas from thoughts or notes into the computer is the fundamental purpose of word processing. The end product is to get the finished document out of the computer in a readable, productive format.

But, back to step one—entering the text into *Microsoft Word*. The New Document screen looks like a standard piece of typing paper and the keyboard is very similar to the old IBM Selectric typewriter. The **Enter** (Windows) or **Return** (Macintosh) key has replaced the carriage return key on the typewriter. Several extra keys populate the keyboard as well: **Ctrl**, **Alt**, **Esc**, **Delete**, **Insert**, **Home**, **End**, and others. Each has a unique purpose and contributes to the functionality of the computer program.

Note the flashing vertical line. This is the insertion point; the place where the letters will appear when typed. As your mouse moves over the blank page, it looks like an upper case "I." Another name for this line is the I-beam.

Try This:

- Type the following sentence:

(The birds are singing in the old oak tree while the rain falls gently on the newly mowed grass.)

- Do not press the **Enter** (Windows) or **Return** (Macintosh) key after the word (falls). The word processing program will automatically decide where a new line begins. When you are finished typing the sentence, the flashing vertical line will be positioned directly after the period at the end of the sentence.

- Now, take your mouse and use it to point the I-beam at the word (singing) and click your mouse (Macintosh) or the left button on your mouse (Windows). Notice that the insertion point is now flashing in the word (*singing*) instead of at the end of the sentence.

Tips for Success:

- Practice good posture while entering text into the computer, and use proper lighting.

- Do not press the **Enter** (Windows) or **Return** (Macintosh) key at the end of the line. *Microsoft Word* will automatically go to the next line if the line is wider than the page. Press **Enter** or **Return** at the end of a paragraph to move the cursor to the next line.

- Use one blank space after commas and two after periods.

Fonts and Font Size

Microsoft Word gives you the ability to change the typeface and size of the characters or fonts in your document. You can have a great time selecting the font that will compliment your document or project. Not all computers have the same fonts installed into their font folders. The following are examples of different fonts.

Formal invitations might use ShelleyVolante:

You are cordially invited to the celebration . . .

An appropriate font for a barn dance might be:

HOG BOLD

Other fun fonts include:

Freestyle Script

Hobo

LITHOS BOLD

tree frog

You can also change the size of your fonts for emphasis and style.

Giant

Tiny

Try This:

- Select **FORMAT** from the menu bar.

- Choose *Font* from the drop down menu.

- Click the first Font name in the **Font** box.

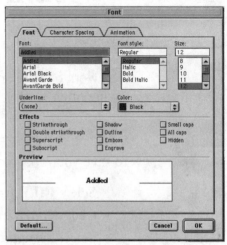

- Use your down arrow to scroll through the names. As you select a font style, notice that a sample of that font is shown in the preview window.

- In the Size box, click the size of font you wish to use. These can also be previewed in the window.

- Click the **OK** button when you have selected the right font and size for your project.

- If you are using a Macintosh platform, **FONT** is also an option on your menu bar. Simply click **FONT** and scroll through the different styles.

Tips for Success:

- Have fun and be creative.

- Select a font that is readable. Several of the unusual fonts are difficult to read and may detract from the reader's understanding of your document.

- Use a size 12 font for handouts and a size 36 font for overhead transparencies if at all possible. These are recommended minimums; however, larger or smaller fonts may be necessary for some projects.

  Note: You can also change the font and font size from your Formatting toolbar.

Saving Your Document

If you wish to save your document for future use, to make changes, or to print the document again, you will need to save your work on the hard drive of your computer or on a diskette. Saving often is very important!

Try This:

To save your document (Windows):

- Select **FILE** from the menu bar.
- Choose *Save* from the drop down menu.
- Select the appropriate folder using the **Save in** box.

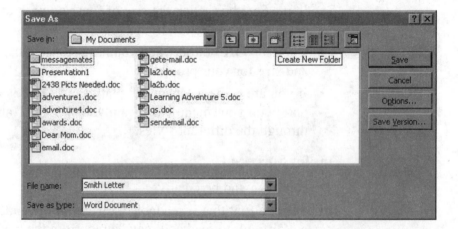

- Enter the name of the document in the **File name** box.
- Click the **Save** button.

Try This:

To save your document (Macintosh):

- Select **FILE** from the menu bar.
- Choose *Save* from the drop down menu.
- Open the Macintosh hard drive and choose the appropriate folder or create a new folder using the **New Folder** button.
- Enter the name of the document in the **Save Current Document as**: box.
- Click the **Save** button.

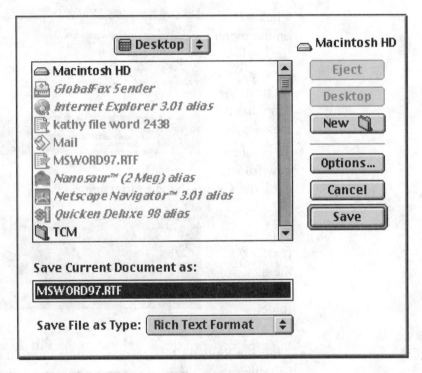

Your document has just been filed on your computer's hard drive.

Tips for Success:

Create a new folder for each type of work or project so that you can easily find your document in the future. For example:

Letters	Notes to Parents
Invitations	Newsletters
Back to School Project	

Try This:

To create a new folder (Windows):

- Click **FILE** on the menu bar, and choose *Save As* from the drop down menu.

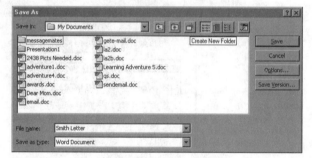

- To create a new folder, click the **Create New Folder** button:

- Click **Name**.

- Type in (*Letters*) as the name of the new folder.

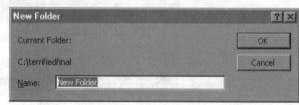

- Click the **OK** button.

- After the **Save As** box appears, select the folder (*Letters*), and click the **Open** button.

- Click the **Save** button. Your document is now saved in the folder (*Letters*).

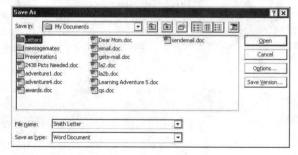

To create a new folder (Macintosh):

- Click **FILE** on the menu bar, and choose *Save As* from the drop down menu.
- Create a new folder by selecting the **New Folder** button.
- A dialog box will appear and ask you to type a name into the **Name of new folder:** box.
- Name your new folder (*Letters*) and click the **Create** button.
- The new folder name will appear at the top of the **Save As** dialog box as the location where you will be saving this document.
- Click the **Save** button. Your document is now saved in the (*Letters*) folder.

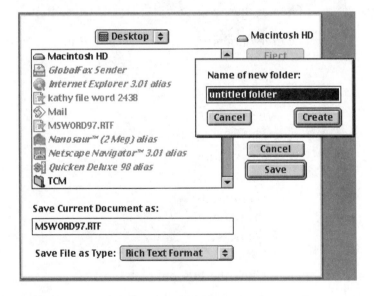

 Tips for Success:

Give your work names that clearly describe what is contained in the document. Use the most descriptive word first in the name so that you can recognize the contents of the document. If you write to Tom Smith on a regular basis, you may wish to change the name of your document to *(Smith Letter Requesting Appointment)*. Placing the date in the file name can also be helpful, such as, *(Smith Letter Requesting Appointment 12-01-98)*.

One of the new features of *Windows 95, Windows 98,* and *Windows NT* allows for long file names. You can use up to 255 characters including spaces and the name of the folder where the document is filed.

Windows reserves certain characters that you cannot use in your file names. *Microsoft Word* will also tell you if there is a problem.

The following characters cannot be used in file names:

Back Slash	/	Forward Slash	\
Colon	:	Semicolon	;
Asterisk	*	Question Mark	?
Greater than	>	Less than	<
Double quotes	"	Pipe	|

Saving Your Work under a Different Name or Location

As you work on your projects, you will want to save your work often. Sometimes the electricity will go out or your computer will misbehave and, if you have not saved your work for an hour, everything you did for the last sixty minutes will be lost.

At times, you will add graphics and effects to your documents that do not look exactly as you had planned. A good technique for insuring that you can always get back to the original document is to save the file under a different name.

Your document may be saved as (*Smith Letter*). Your backup copy may be saved as (*Smith Letter Copy*).

Try This:

- Choose **FILE** from the menu bar.
- Select *Save As* from the drop down menu.
- Click in the **File name** box after the word (Letter).
- Space and type (Copy).
- Click the **Save** button.

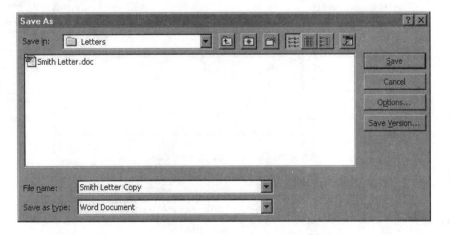

You may wish to save your work to a diskette so that you can work on it at home or on another computer.

Try This:

To save your document on a disk (Windows):

- Click the **Up One Level** button until you see **My Computer** in the **Save** window.
- Select the icon labeled **3½ Floppy (A:)** to save to a diskette. Be sure that a disk is in the drive before clicking A:.
- Type the name you want to call this file into the **Filename** window.
- Click the **Save** button.

To save your document on a disk (Macintosh):

- From the **Save As** dialog box, double click the floppy disk icon from the desktop window.
- The disk will open and you can name your file in the **Save Current Document as:** window.
- Click the **Save** button.

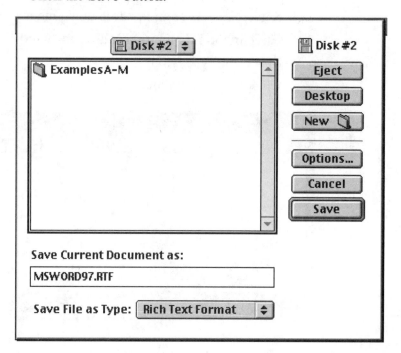

Using the Spell Check

Microsoft Word provides you with the option to continuously spell check your documents as you create them.

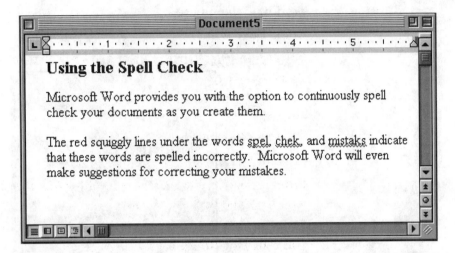

The red squiggly lines under the words *spel, chek,* and *mistaks* indicate that these words are spelled incorrectly. *Microsoft Word* will make suggestions for correcting your mistakes.

Try This:

- (Windows) Point your cursor at the error and click using the right button on your mouse. A dialog box will appear with a list of correct spellings suggested.
- (Macintosh) Hold down the **control** key and click on the word with the mouse.

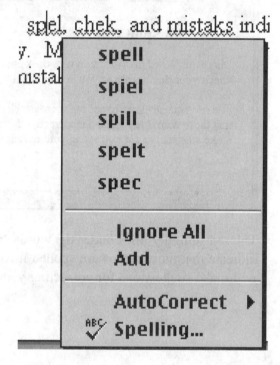

- Select and click the correct word with the left mouse button.
- If the word is actually spelled correctly, but is not contained in the *Microsoft Word* dictionary, it will also be marked with the red line. To keep the word as it is spelled, select **Ignore All** with the left mouse button.
- If the word is not contained in the *Microsoft Word* dictionary but you use it on a regular basis, such as the name of your school, add it to the dictionary by clicking **Add** with the left mouse button.

- (Macintosh) Highlight the misspelled word.
- Click the **ABC√** button on the toolbar or click **TOOLS** from the menu bar, and select *Spelling and Grammar* from the drop down menu.

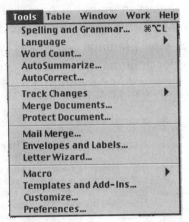

- A dialog box will appear with the sentence or fragment of the sentence which contains the misspelled word in the **Not in Dictionary:** box. There will also be suggestions for spelling the word correctly in the **Suggestions:** box.
- Select the correct spelling of the word that is in your document and click the **Change** button.

- If the word is actually spelled correctly, but is not contained in the *Microsoft Word* dictionary, it will also be marked with the red line. To keep the word as it is spelled, select **Ignore All** with the mouse button.
- If the word is not contained in the *Microsoft Word* dictionary but you use it on a regular basis, such as the name of your school, add it to the dictionary by clicking **Add** with the mouse button.

Tips for Success:

Proofread, proofread, and proofread! *Microsoft Word* does not know what you intend to say. It can only determine if the words you typed match words within its dictionary. Remember, both "led" and "lead" are spelled correctly. Which is the right word? It depends on the sentence and what you are trying to say.

Using the Grammar Check

Unfortunately for most of us, it has been a long time since we took a class in grammar or even reviewed basic grammar rules. With *Microsoft Word*, this is not a problem. *Microsoft Word* will check your grammar for you as you create your document. If you use poor grammar or incorrect sentence structures, *Microsoft Word* will let you know by putting a green squiggly line beneath the problem area.

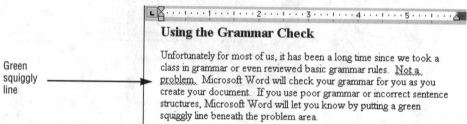

Using the Grammar Check

Unfortunately for most of us, it has been a long time since we took a class in grammar or even reviewed basic grammar rules. Not a problem. Microsoft Word will check your grammar for you as you create your document. If you use poor grammar or incorrect sentence structures, Microsoft Word will let you know by putting a green squiggly line beneath the problem area.

Green squiggly line

Try This:

- To find out what *Microsoft Word* considers the problem, point at the underlined word or phrase with the mouse and click with the right button (Windows) or highlight the word or phrase and choose ***Spelling and Grammar*** from the **TOOLS** drop down menu (Macintosh).

- Now you have a decision to make. In formal writing, you will always want to use the strictest rules of grammar. However, for a conversational tone, you can choose to ignore *Microsoft Word*'s suggestion. You will then point and click at **Ignore Sentence** with your left mouse button (Windows) or click **Ignore** (Macintosh).

- To look at a word usage problem, type the sentence *(The book fall on the ground.)*
- Use either the Windows or Macintosh option to check the grammar of this sentence.

- Select the correction of your choice from the list of options and click. The correction will be made automatically.

Microsoft Word gives you two additional ways to access the check grammar feature.

- Select the sentence or phrase you would like to check.
- From your toolbar, click the **ABC√** button.

  or

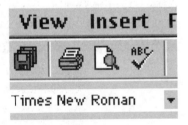

- Select the sentence or phrase you would like to check.
- Select **TOOLS** from your menu bar.
- Click the *Spelling and Grammar* option.

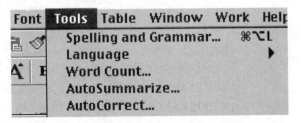

Tips for Success:

At times, you might want to type worksheets that intentionally have mistakes, and you may wish to turn off the check grammar feature. To do this:

- Select **TOOLS** from your menu bar.
- Click the *Spelling and Grammar* option.
- When the dialog box appears, point and click in the **Check grammar** box. The check mark will disappear and the automatic check grammar feature will be turned off.

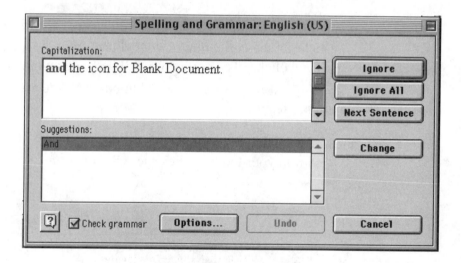

Counting Words

How many times have you been asked to write a description of a project or activity in one hundred words or less? So you sit down and count, and count, and count. *Microsoft Word* gives you a tool for counting words.

Try This:

- To count the words in a whole document, select **TOOLS** from your menu bar.
- Click the ***Word Count*** option. This will give you a count of all of the words in the whole document.

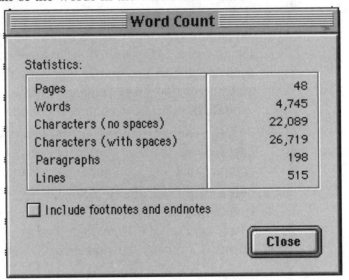

Word Count

Statistics:

Pages	48
Words	4,745
Characters (no spaces)	22,089
Characters (with spaces)	26,719
Paragraphs	198
Lines	515

☐ Include footnotes and endnotes

Close

Tips for Success:

To count the words in a section of your document, select the text you wish to count before choosing ***Word Count*** from the **TOOLS** menu.

Note: *Microsoft Word* has an option for including or excluding footnotes and endnotes from the word count.

AutoCorrect

Wouldn't it be nice if someone followed you around to fix those little mistakes that we all make when rushing through a project? *Microsoft Word* watches each word you type. It will automatically take care of some of the words that are occasionally mistyped or when the first letter of a sentence does not get capitalized. It will not do everything, but it certainly can help. Here is what it will do:

1. AutoCorrect will capitalize the names of days automatically. Just try to type Wednesday without a capital. With AutoCorrect on, *Microsoft Word* will not allow you to do it.

2. AutoCorrect will capitalize the first letter of a sentence. When you type the first letter of a line after a return or at the top of a page, *Microsoft Word* assumes that you are writing a sentence and will capitalize that word for you. AutoCorrect also knows that a new sentence follows a period and capitalizes the first word after a period.

3. AutoCorrect corrects two capital letters followed by a lower case letter at the beginning of a word. *Microsoft Word* assumes that you left your finger on the shift key a bit too long and changes the second capital to lower case.

4. If your word begins with a lower case letter and all other letters are capitals, *Microsoft Word* assumes you left the Caps Lock on and fixes the error by switching the cases.

5. AutoCorrect automatically corrects commonly misspelled words. Take a look at the words AutoCorrect currently has in its list.

Try This:

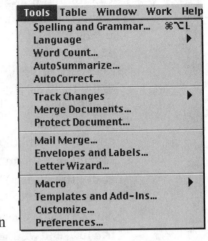

- Select **TOOLS** from your menu bar.
- Click the *AutoCorrect* function.

Microsoft Word includes a large list of words that are often misspelled, and symbols that are commonly substituted. If you misspell the word as it is shown in AutoCorrect, *Microsoft Word* will change your entry to the correct spelling. You can add your own problem words to the list.

Try This:

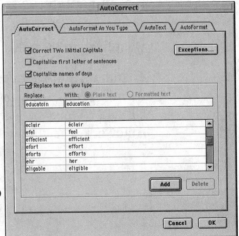

- In the **Replace text as you type** box, type in the word as you commonly misspell it in the **Replace** box.
- Type the correct spelling in the **With** box.
- Click the **Add** button.
- Click the **OK** button to close AutoCorrect.

Tips for Success:

AutoCorrect will do exactly what you tell it to do. Therefore, be careful and make sure your entry in the **With** box is absolutely correct. Do not add a word that is the correct spelling of another word.

AutoCorrect can add symbols to your documents as well. You can add the copyright symbol or several other symbols easily to your documents with AutoCorrect. Do your friends send you letters with a happy face in the middle of their sentences? Now you know their secret; it is in AutoCorrect.

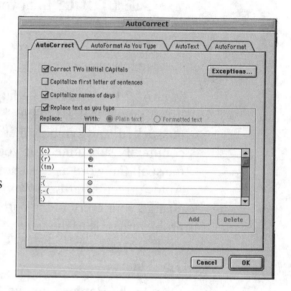

If you are teaching word processing to your students, you may not want them to have this much assistance in performing their tasks.

To turn off AutoCorrect, select the check boxes at the top of the **AutoCorrect** box with your mouse and click (Macintosh) the left button (Windows). The checkmark will disappear, and that AutoCorrect feature will be turned off.

Tips for Success:

You can add entries to AutoCorrect as you check your spelling.

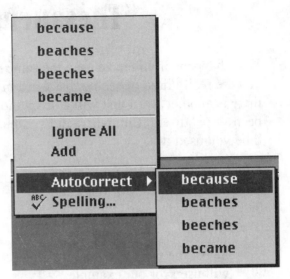

- Point and right click the misspelled word (Windows) or double-click (Macintosh).
- Click the **ABC√** button on the toolbar (Macintosh).
- Click the **AutoCorrect** button.
- Click the correct spelling. The error with its correction has now been added to the AutoCorrect file.

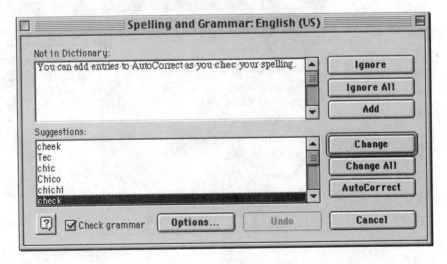

What is Another Word for "Thesaurus"?

What happens if you have used the same word over and over, and you are really tired of seeing that word in your document? Surely there is another word that will convey the meaning that has not been so overused. But, where did you put the thesaurus the last time you used it?

Microsoft Word's Thesaurus gives you a world of words at your fingertips. Here is how to use it.

Try This:

- Select the word you want to replace. The word (replace) will used for our example.
- Select **TOOLS** from your menu bar.
- Click *Language* from the drop down menu.
- Choose *Thesaurus* from the next drop down menu.

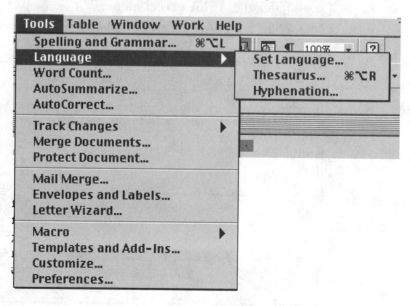

- Select the correct meaning from the **Meanings:** box for the word you want to replace.
- Select the word you want to use from the **Replace with Synonym:** box.
- Click the **Replace** button.

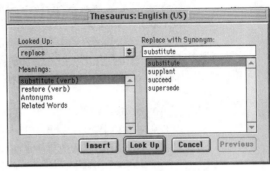

Now the sentence reads *(Select the word you want to substitute.)*

Tips for Success:

You can also find an antonym for a word in the thesaurus. Click the **Antonym** choice and a list will appear in the **Replace with Antonym:** box.

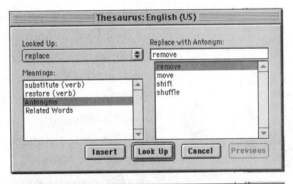

Another option of the *Microsoft Word* Thesaurus, is a list of **Related Words:** words that are similar to or related to the selected word.

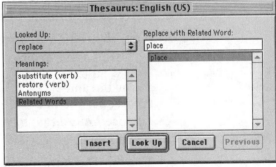

Activity #1: In Other Words

Microsoft Word can help you discover new words to use in your documents that convey the same meaning. Add variety to your writing by adding variety to your vocabulary.

- Start *Microsoft Word* by clicking **Start**, choosing **Programs**, then choosing *Microsoft Word* (Windows) or double-clicking the *Microsoft Word* icon in the *Microsoft Office* folder (Macintosh).
- Once *Microsoft Word* is on your screen, choose *New* from the **FILE** drop down menu, and then select the icon for **Blank Document**.
- Type the following sentences into the new document:

  1. If a good policeman is able to **lead** effectively, does he use **lead** in his gun?
  2. How can you have a barn raising, yet when a building is imploded it is **raised**?
  3. The item was not marked, but certainly did not appear **priceless**.
  4. Can there be another word for **unique** or would that make it **common**?
  5. The material was **flammable**, but the label said "**Inflammable** Material." Which is right?
  6. Mr. Wells was a **material** witness in the case of the stolen **material**.
  7. We finally reached the **finale** of the Finnish festival of fine furniture finishes.

- Choose *Language*, then *Thesaurus*, from the **TOOLS** drop down menu.
- Use the Thesaurus to find the bolded words and their alternative meanings.

Closing a Document

You have worked hard, entered your text, corrected spelling errors, and proofread the document. You have carefully saved your work on your computer's hard drive, and now it is time for a well-deserved break. First, you will need to close your document.

Try This:

- Select **FILE** from the menu bar.
- Choose *Close* from the drop down menu.
- Then *Microsoft Word* says, "Wait just a minute." It gives you a last chance to save any changes in the document that have not previously been saved.

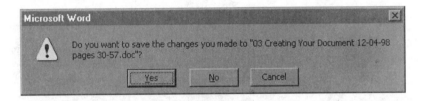

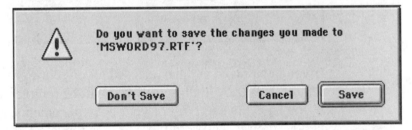

- Click the **Yes** button (Windows) or the **Save** button (Macintosh). Your document will close and leave you at the blank *Microsoft Word* screen.

Tips for Success:

You may wish to close *Microsoft Word* without saving your last changes. If so, click the **No** button (Windows) or **Don't Save** button (Macintosh) when asked, and the stored document will remain as it was originally filed.

Exiting Microsoft Word

Before you turn off your computer and sit back to relax, you will need to exit *Microsoft Word*. Exiting *Microsoft Word* is different from just closing the application. When you choose **Close** from the **FILE** drop down menu, you are simply closing the document in which you are currently working. The application, *Microsoft Word*, is still running. When you choose **Exit** (Windows) or **Quit** (Macintosh), you are exiting completely out of the application.

Try This:

- Select **FILE** from the menu bar.
- Choose **Exit** (Windows) or **Quit** (Macintosh) from the drop down menu.

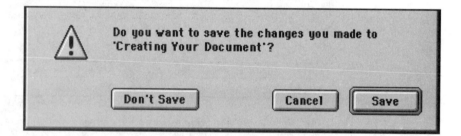

Do you want to save the changes you made to 'Creating Your Document'?

Don't Save   Cancel   Save

If you have saved and have closed all of your open documents, *Microsoft Word* will close and you will be returned to the desktop. If you have not saved all of your open documents, *Microsoft Word* will ask you if you would like to save the latest changes. Click **Yes** (Windows) or **Save** (Macintosh) to save the changes, **No** (Windows) or **Don't Save** (Macintosh) to discard the changes. If you are not really ready to exit *Microsoft Word*, click **Cancel**.

Activity #2: A Note to Parents

How many notes do you send home to parents each year? Practice all that you have learned by writing a reminder note of an upcoming event.

1. Start *Microsoft Word* by clicking **Start**, choosing **Programs**, then choosing *Microsoft Word* (Windows) or double-click the *Microsoft Word* icon in the *Microsoft Office* folder (Macintosh).

2. Once *Microsoft Word* is on your screen, choose *New* from the **FILE** drop down menu (Macintosh) or select the icon for Blank Document (Windows).

3. Type the following note into *Microsoft Word*. Remember to press **Enter** (Windows) or **Return** (Macintosh) only when you need to start a new line, such as in the heading and between paragraphs. *Microsoft Word* will automatically go to the next line when the sentence is longer than the width of the page.

Field Days

May 6, 7, and 8

Our class will be competing in Field Days on Tuesday, May 6. The class voted to wear blue t-shirts and blue jean shorts as our class uniform. Please have your student wear shoes appropriate for running races.

You are invited to watch our class compete and cheer us on to victory.

Thank you for your support. See you on the 6th.

- Check for spelling errors. Do you see any red squiggly lines? If so, point and click the word with the right mouse button. Select the correct spelling by clicking the word with the left mouse button (Windows). Or highlight the misspelled word and click the **ABC√** button on the toolbar or click **TOOLS** from the menu bar and select *Spelling and Grammar* from the drop down menu. Select the correct spelling and click the **Change** button (Macintosh).
- Save your document by choosing *Save* from the **FILE** drop down menu. Type in the name of the document (Note to Parents). Click the **Save** button again.
- Exit *Microsoft Word* by selecting *Exit* (Windows) or *Quit* (Macintosh) from the **FILE** menu.

A job well done! Congratulations!

You have just completed your first *Microsoft Word* document.

See an example on the CD-ROM (56act2.doc).

Now, where is that glass of iced tea?

Opening a File

Now that you have had a chance to catch your breath and drink that iced tea, you are ready to revisit your first document and make some changes.

Try This:

- To retrieve the document that you saved earlier, click **FILE** from the menu bar.
- Choose *Open* from the drop down menu.
- Select the file *(Note to Parents)*, and click the **Open** button.

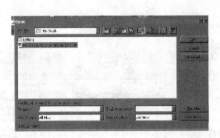 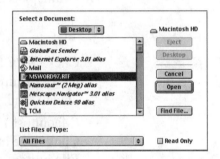

Now your document is open and ready for you to go to work.

Tips for Success:

You may also access your stored files by using the **Open Folder** button on your toolbar.

Finding a Document When You Can't Remember What You Named It

You have worked all day and most of the night to create your masterpiece. It looks wonderful! So you carefully file it on the hard drive of your computer for safekeeping, and off to bed you go. The next morning you start to look for the file. Where did you file it? What did you name it? Here is an easy way to look for your misplaced file.

Try This:

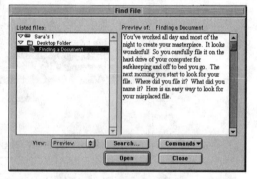

- Click *Open* from the **FILE** drop down menu.

- (Macintosh) Click the **Find File** button.

- Type part of the file name in the **File name** box.

- Click the **Find Now** (Windows) or **OK** button (Macintosh).

If found, the file will be highlighted and then you can click the **Open** button. To clear out the fields so that you can start a new search, click the **New Search** (Windows) or **Search** button (Macintosh). For more complex searches, click the **Advanced** (Windows) or **Advanced Search** button (Macintosh).

Selecting Text

Selecting text means that you highlight specific words. To do this, point at the first word with the cursor, hold down the mouse button, and drag the arrow to the end of the area you wish to select. This may sound pretty complicated, but it is really quite easy.

Try This:

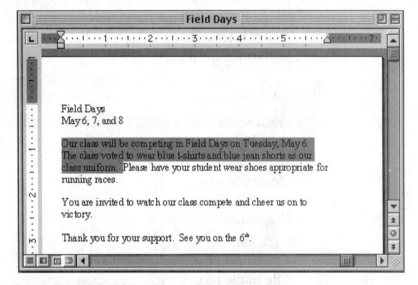

- Point your cursor before the word *(Our)* in your *(Note to Parents)* document. Press the mouse button (Macintosh) or the left mouse button (Windows).

- Drag the mouse to the right and down one row. Let go of the mouse button after the word *(uniform).* Notice how this area is now highlighted. This area is referred to as a selection or selected text.

Tips for Success:

To select a word, place your cursor on the word with the mouse and click the mouse button (Macintosh) or the left mouse button (Windows) twice quickly.

- To select an entire paragraph, place your cursor in the paragraph and click the mouse button (Macintosh) or the left mouse button (Windows) quickly three times.
- To select the remainder of a line, hold down **Shift** and press the **End** key on your keyboard.
- To select a letter at a time, hold down **Shift** and press the **Right** or **Left Arrow** key on your keyboard.
- To select a large area of text, point the mouse in the left margin, and the mouse pointer will become an arrow. Hold down the mouse button (Macintosh) or the left mouse button (Windows) and drag straight down the page. Release the mouse button. You can see that the area that you have selected is now highlighted.

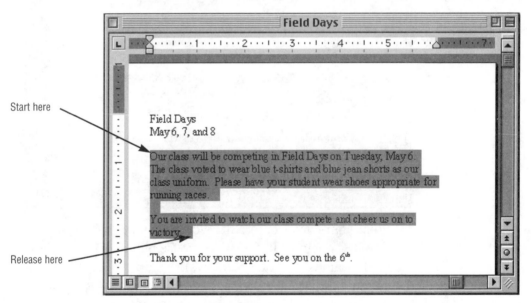

- To select a line, place your mouse arrow in the left margin next to the line and click the mouse button (Macintosh) or the left mouse button (Windows) once.

- To select a paragraph, place your mouse arrow in the left margin next to the paragraph and click the mouse button (Macintosh) or the left mouse button (Windows) twice.
- To select the entire document, place your mouse arrow in the left margin and click the mouse button (Macintosh) or the left mouse button (Windows) three times.

Microsoft Word also will let you select the entire document by:

- Click **EDIT** from the menu bar.
- Click *Select All* from the drop down menu.

Selection Area	Action to be Taken
Word	Left click (Windows) or click (Macintosh) two times.
Paragraph	Left click (Windows) or click (Macintosh) three times.
Sentence	**Ctrl** + Left click three times (Windows) or ⌘ + click once (Macintosh).
To end of line	**Shift + End**.
One letter at a time	**Ctrl** (Windows) or **Shift** (Macintosh) + **Right** or **Left Arrow**.
One line	Left click (Windows) or click (Macintosh) in left margin.
One Paragraph	Left click (Windows) or click (Macintosh) twice in left margin.
Entire document	Left click (Windows) or click (Macintosh) three times in left margin.
Entire document	**EDIT** and then *Select All*.

Take a moment now and practice all of your new selection techniques. As you learn to copy, delete, move, and format your documents, selection of text will become one of your most useful tools in *Microsoft Word*.

Help! I Didn't Mean to Do That.

Did you ever throw out a treasured possession and wish you could get it back? Or, did you ever paint a room a color that did not look anything like you thought it would?

Microsoft Word has an option that will let you undo typing, deletions, pastes, and formatting. If you do not like how one of your revisions looks, or if it did not really work the way you thought it would, you can use *Microsoft Word*'s **Undo** function to take you back to where you were before.

Try This:

- To use **Undo**, click **EDIT** from the menu bar.
- Select *Undo* from the drop down menu. Your last action will be reversed.

Tips for Success:

Undo will only work in the current session of *Microsoft Word* for the current document! Once you have saved a file, closed a file, or exited *Microsoft Word*, you can no longer use Undo for any work prior to those actions.

If you undo something that you wish you had not, you can use *Microsoft Word*'s **Repeat** feature. Select *Repeat* from the **EDIT** drop down menu. Now you know how to undo your undo.

Undo and **Redo** are also available on your toolbar. They appear as curled left and curled right arrows.

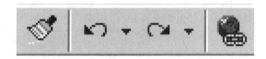

Cut, Copy, and Paste

Remember back in the good ole days when you would type a letter and then notice that it really would sound better if the paragraphs were in another order? Well, the good ole days were not really all that good, because rearranging those paragraphs meant retyping the whole letter.

With *Microsoft Word*, you can rearrange, copy, and move words, sentences, paragraphs, and pictures. Just about anything you can put into a *Microsoft Word* document can be cut, copied, or pasted.

Try This:

- To Cut (erase or delete) a selection, select the word or phrase you wish to remove.
- Select **EDIT** from the menu bar.
- Choose *Cut* from the drop down menu.

The selection disappears. *Microsoft Word* holds this selection in its memory temporarily in case you want to place it in another location. This temporary location is called the clipboard.

Edit	View	Insert	Fi
Undo Typing		⌘Z	
Repeat Typing		⌘Y	
Cut		⌘X	
Copy		⌘C	
Paste		⌘V	
Paste Special...			
Paste as Hyperlink			
Clear			
Select All		⌘A	
Find...		⌘F	
Replace...		⌘H	
Go To...		⌘G	
Links...			
Object			
Publishing		▶	

To paste a selection, means to take the information out of the temporary memory and put it back into your document.

Try This:

- To Paste the selection in a new location, use your mouse to move the cursor to the area where you want the copied selection to be placed and click.
- Select **EDIT** from the menu bar.
- Choose *Paste* from the drop down menu.

At times you may want words or parts of your document to be repeated throughout your document. For example, if you have typed a note to the parents on the top half of the paper, you can simply copy that information to the bottom half instead of retyping the note. You have saved paper, and you have saved yourself some valuable time!

Try This:

- To Copy, select the word or phrase you wish to cut.
- Select **EDIT** from the menu bar.
- Choose *Copy* from the drop down menu.
- Use your mouse to move the cursor to the area where you want the copied selection to be placed and click.
- Select **EDIT** from the menu bar.
- Choose *Paste* from the drop down menu.

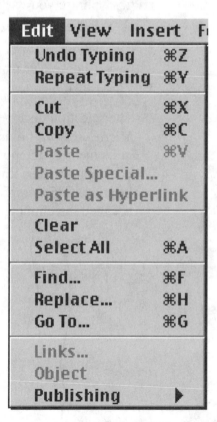

Tips for Success:

Microsoft Word will only keep your last Cut or Copy selection in its temporary memory or clipboard.

Cut, **Copy**, and **Paste** are available on your toolbar. They appear as a pair of scissors (Cut), two sheets of paper (Copy), and a clipboard and piece of paper (Paste).

In addition to your menus and toolbar, *Microsoft Word* lets you do many actions through the keyboard with a combination of keystrokes. After selecting the text:

To **Cut**, press **Ctrl** (Windows) or ⌘ (Macintosh) + **X**.

To **Copy**, press **Ctrl** (Windows) or ⌘ (Macintosh) + **C**.

To **Paste**, press **Ctrl** (Windows) or ⌘ (Macintosh) + **V**.

You will learn more about copying, deleting, and moving text in the next section.

Activity #3: A Note to Parents Revisited

For this activity, use the skills you have just learned and do a little rearranging on your (Note to Parents). You have decided that your introductory paragraph should be more of an invitation to encourage parents to attend the Field Day activities.

Note: The sentences to be moved are highlighted.

Field Days

May 6, 7, and 8

Our class will be competing in Field Days on Tuesday, May 6. The class voted to wear blue t-shirts and blue jean shorts as our class uniform. Please have your student wear shoes appropriate for running races.

You are invited to watch our class compete and cheer us on to victory.

Thank you for your support. See you on the 6th.

Field Days

May 6, 7, and 8

Our class will be competing in Field Days on Tuesday, May 6. You are invited to watch our class compete and cheer us on to victory.

The class voted to wear blue t-shirts and blue jean shorts as our class uniform. Please have your student wear shoes appropriate for running races.

Thank you for your support. See you on the 6th.

- Open your (Note to Parents) file, by selecting ***Open*** from the **FILE** drop down menu.
- Select the sentences beginning with (The class voted to wear . . .) and (Please have your student . . .)
- Select ***Cut*** from the **EDIT** drop down menu.
- Point your mouse to the line above the last sentence, and click ***Paste*** from the **EDIT** menu. Go to the end of the sentence that ends in *(races.)* and press **Enter** (Windows) or **Return** (Macintosh) to insert a blank line between the paragraphs.
- Now select the sentence beginning with *(You are invited . . .)* by placing your mouse pointer anywhere in the sentence and press **Ctrl** and click the left mouse button (Windows) or and click the mouse (Macintosh). Move the sentence to the clipboard by selecting ***Cut*** from the **EDIT** drop down menu.
- Place the I-beam after the period following (May 6) and space once, then click **EDIT**, and then **Paste**.

See an example on the CD-ROM (67act3.doc).

Viola! Way to go!

Inserting Text

In the previous activity, you had an opportunity to insert sentences that you had cut from other areas of the document. Now you will look at inserting text that has not already been entered.

First of all, how do you know where to place the I-beam, also know as the insertion point? (A convenient name, don't you think?) Place the I-beam at the exact location where you want to start entering new text. Here are several considerations that you should keep in mind.

Try This:

- Place the I-beam between two characters to add additional letters or a space. The new character will be inserted as you type. Notice how *Microsoft Word* moves the entire line of text and even makes the decision when to wrap or continue the sentence to a new line.

- To insert a blank line between paragraphs, place the I-beam directly before the first letter in the next sentence of the new paragraph and press **Enter** (Windows) or **Return** (Macintosh).

- Position the I-beam anywhere within a paragraph and press **Enter** (Windows) or **Return** (Macintosh) twice to break it into two paragraphs.

- Note that the extra **Enter** or **Return** left a blank line between the paragraphs.
- To insert a blank space on the page, simply press **Enter** (Windows) or **Return** (Macintosh) several times and watch as the text below the insertion point moves down the page.

Remember those strange little characters that were discussed earlier? If you want to see how many blank lines you have entered into your document, click the **Show/Hide** button on your toolbar and a ¶ symbol will appear for each time that you have pressed **Enter** or **Return.** To remove all of those little symbols, click the **Show/Hide** button again.

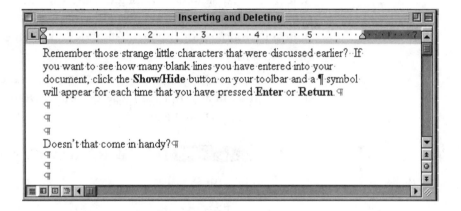

Tips for Success:

If you make an insertion or change that does not look right to you, you can use the **Undo** feature to get you back to where you started.

Moving Text

Earlier you learned that *Microsoft Word* lets you move text by cutting and pasting. It will also allow you to move blocks of text by simply selecting the text and dragging it to a new location.

Try This:

- To practice moving a sentence from the beginning to the end of a paragraph, type the following sentences: *(The house is yellow. Look for the third house on the left.)*

- Select the first sentence by placing the I-beam over the first sentence and pressing **Ctrl** and clicking the left mouse button (Windows) or pressing ⌘ and clicking the mouse (Macintosh).

- Place the I-beam over the selected area and hold down the mouse (Macintosh) or left mouse button (Windows). The I-beam will turn into an arrow.

> The house is yellow. Look for the third house on the left

- Now, drag the selection to the end of the next sentence and release the mouse button.

> Look for the third house on the left The house is yellow.

Tips for Success:

Remember the **Undo** button if you do not like the move!

Copying Text

Microsoft Word gives you another method for copying text from one part of a document to another other than **Copy** and **Paste**.

Try This:

- Type the next few lines into *Microsoft Word*:

  (Name:
  Address:
  Telephone:)

- To copy these lines, select the three lines by pointing before the N in *(Name),* pressing your mouse button (Macintosh) or left mouse button (Windows) and dragging it through the colon after *(Telephone:).*

- Place your I-beam anywhere over the selection.

- Hold down the **Ctrl** key (Windows) or the **Option** key (Macintosh) on your keyboard, then click and hold down your mouse button (Macintosh) or left mouse button (Windows). The I-beam becomes an arrow.

- Drag the mouse to a new location, and release the mouse button. The words have now been copied to another location.

Activity #4: All Mixed Up

This is a little story you can use to practice your inserting and deleting skills.

Type the following paragraphs:

(Once upon a time, in the World of Wonder, there lived a little mouse in a small tiny house. Everything was shiny and new in this house and it was the pride and joy of the little mouse.

One day, a mean cat sauntered through the yard and spied the little house. "What a bother," he thought. Why did he get that house? The cat couldn't believe that he deserved a house.)

Now do the following to the paragraph:

1. Move the word *(mean)* from the second paragraph to in front of the first *(little)*.
2. Move the word *(tiny)* to describe the cat.
3. In the last sentence, delete *(cat)* and insert *(mouse)*.
4. Delete the word *(spied)* and put *(invaded)* in its place.
5. Move the last sentence in the first paragraph to the last sentence in the last paragraph.
6. Delete the word *(couldn't)*.
7. Insert a *(d)* at the end of the word *(believe)*.

The more you practice cut and paste, copy, move, and insert, the easier it becomes!

Backspace and Delete Keys

The **Backspace** (Windows) or **Delete** (Macintosh) key on your keyboard works very much as it did on the old typewriter. If you type a word incorrectly, simply press the **Backspace** or **Delete** key and a letter will be erased with each press of the key.

Backspace (Windows) or **Delete** (Macintosh) is used to delete letters to the left of the insertion point.

Delete (Windows) or Del (Macintosh) Key

The **Delete** (Windows) or **Del** (Macintosh) key allows you to delete characters after the insertion point. If you need to remove some letters after the insertion point, click the mouse in the right location to place the I-beam, and press the **Delete** or **Del** key for each letter you wish to remove.

Delete (Windows) or **Del** (Macintosh) is used to delete letters to the right of the insertion point.

Deleting Words

- To delete words to the left of the insertion point, hold down **Ctrl** (Windows) or ⌘ (Macintosh) while pressing the **Backspace** (Windows) or **Delete** (Macintosh) key.
- To delete words to the right of the insertion point, hold down **Ctrl** (Windows) or ⌘ (Macintosh) while pressing the **Delete** (Windows) or **Del** (Macintosh) key.

Deleting Lines

- To delete entire lines select the line you wish to delete by pointing your mouse in the margin just to the left of the line and click the mouse button (Macintosh) or left click the mouse button (Windows).
- Press the **Delete** key and the line disappears.

Deleting Blocks of Text

- You can delete large blocks of text just as easily. Select the block you wish to erase by pointing your mouse in the margin to the left of the block you want to delete. For a paragraph, double-click the mouse button (Macintosh) or the left mouse button (Windows) in the margin, and the paragraph will be highlighted. For a larger block, click in the left margin, hold down the mouse button (Macintosh) or the left mouse button (Windows) and drag it down to the end of the block.
- Press the **Delete** key and, boom, it is gone!

Tips for Success:

Do not forget to use **Undo** if you have deleted something by mistake. The text you remove using **Delete** is not stored in the clipboard and cannot be pasted.

Microsoft Word gives you one more option for deleting text. After selecting the text you wish to delete, select *Clear* from the **EDIT** drop down menu.

Activity #5: Now You See It . . . Now You Don't

On the old typewriter, did you ever feel like you used the backspace key as much as you were typing forward? No problem. Here is a little intentional deleting practice!

Type this paragraph:

(As you can see, from the things in front of you, everything is visible and easy to view. One might say that with 20/20 vision all is clear. However, in the world of magic, all is not clear. All is not within view. Or, what you see may not be what you are seeing. Confusing? It's designed that way.)

1. After the word *(way)* in the last sentence, use your backspace key to remove (way) and type in the words *(to be).*
2. In the first line, select the second phrase and press **Delete**.
3. Double click the word *(not)* in the sentence beginning *(All is not . . .)* and select ***Clear*** from the **EDIT** menu.
4. Change the second sentence to say, *(With 20/20 vision, all is clear.)*

These changes are all pure silliness. To put them back, click the **Undo** button on your toolbar and watch *Microsoft Word* put things back as they were before, one step at a time with each click.

The Arrow, Home, and End Keys

Moving around your document is easy using the **Arrow** keys, **Page Up**, **Page Down**, **Home** and **End** keys. First look at the different ways the Arrow keys can be used.

Your computer keyboard has two sets of **Arrow** keys—the numeric keypad and one independent set of keys. If the **NumLock** is activated, an indicator will show on your keyboard and the **Arrow** keys will not be useable. To make numeric input more efficient, keep the **NumLock** activated. Therefore, the **Arrow** keys to the left of the numeric keypad are the best to use for moving around a document.

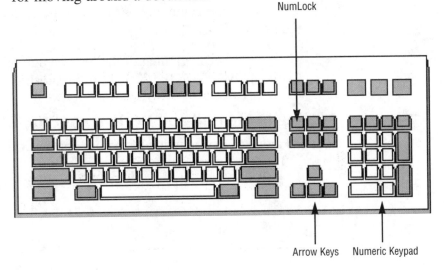

NumLock

Arrow Keys   Numeric Keypad

Try This:

- Moving One Character to the Left or Right:
    1. To move one character to the left, press the → once.
    2. To move one character to the right, press the ← once.

Moving One Line Up or Down:

1. To move up one line, press the ↑ once.

2. To move down one line, press the ↓ once.

Moving One Word to the Left or Right:

1. To move one word to the left, press **Ctrl +** ← (Windows) or ⌘ + ← (Macintosh).

2. To move one word to the right, press **Ctrl +** → (Windows) or ⌘ + → (Macintosh).

Moving to the Beginning of a Paragraph:

1. To move to the beginning of the current paragraph, press **Ctrl +** ↑ (Windows) or ⌘ + ↑ (Macintosh).

2. To move to the beginning of the next paragraph, press **Ctrl +** ↓ (Windows) or ⌘ + ↓ (Macintosh).

Moving to the End and Beginning of the Line:

1. To move to the right end of the line, press **End**.

2. To move to the first of the line, press **Home**.

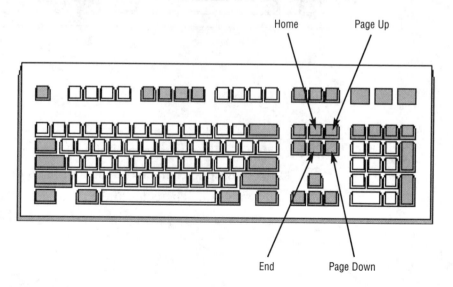

As your documents and projects get larger, you will find that your ability to move up and down throughout the document is very important. *Microsoft Word* gives you several express routes through your document.

Moving a Whole Screen:

1. To move down a whole screen, press **PageDn**.
2. To move up a whole screen, press **PageUp**.

Moving to the Top or Bottom of the Current Screen:

1. To move to the first character on the current screen, press **Ctrl + PageUp** (Windows) or ⌘ **+ PageUp** (Macintosh).
2. To move to the last character of the current screen, press **Ctrl + PageDn** (Windows) or ⌘ **+ PageDn** (Macintosh).

Moving to the Beginning and End of the Document:

1. To move to the beginning of the entire document, press **Ctrl + Home** (Windows) or ⌘ **+ Home** (Macintosh).
2. To move to the end of the entire document, press **Ctrl + End** (Windows) or ⌘ **+ End** (Macintosh).

Using the Scroll Bar

When you look at the *Microsoft Word* screen, you will notice two scroll bars—one on the right side of the screen and one at the bottom. The bar on the right moves the document up and down. The bar on the bottom moves the document to the left and right (if the document is wider than a screen). Both of these functions allow you to move through the document and change the view on your screen.

Try This:

- Click the **Up** and **Down Arrows** to move the document up and down slightly. The document will move about one line per click.
- Click the slide with your mouse (Macintosh) or left mouse button (Windows) and move the document up and down. To work in a new area, place the I-beam in the spot where you want to work and click the mouse or the left mouse button.

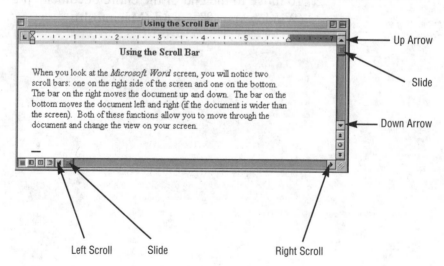

Finding a Single Word

At times, it can be very difficult to find a particular word or phrase in a document by simply scanning the screen. *Microsoft Word* can help you find a word that is buried deep within a document. The **Find** feature will assist you in this task.

Try This:

- To find a word within a document, select **EDIT** from the menu bar.
- Click *Find* from the drop down menu. The **Find** dialog box appears.

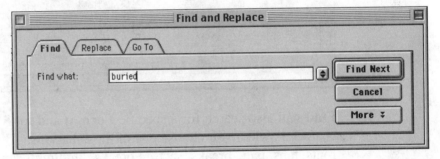

- Type in the word you wish to find.
- Click the **Find Next** button. *Microsoft Word* finds the word that you have requested. It will find the first occurrence of the search word after where your insertion point is located.

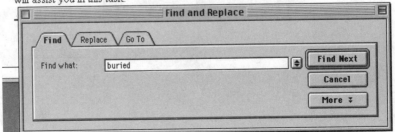

Tips for Success:

You can narrow the scope of your search or broaden the search by using the options that appear at the bottom of the dialog box when you click the **More** button.

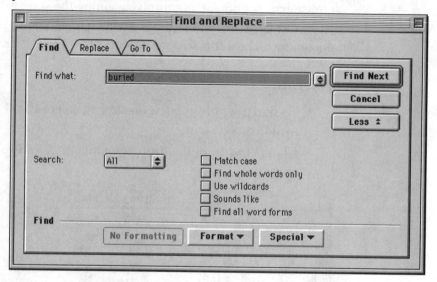

Find will also search for a specific **Format** and for **Special** characters when you choose one of those buttons. This includes fonts, tabs, page breaks, section breaks, highlights, and most of *Microsoft Word*'s other special features.

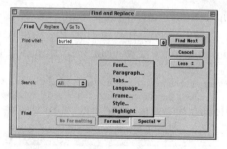

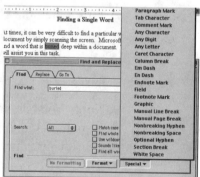

Using Go To

A handy tool is the **Go To** feature in *Microsoft Word*. If you are working on a long document and need to go directly to page 76, you do not have to use **PageDn** or the scroll bar. You can ask *Microsoft Word* to take you directly to page 76.

Try This:

- Select **EDIT** from the menu bar.
- Click *Go To* from the drop down menu. The **Find and Replace** dialog box appears with the **Go To** tab selected.

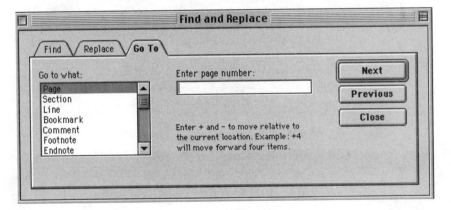

Tips for Success:

You can use a (+) or (−) sign with a number to allow you to look forward and backward in the document a specific number of pages.

Note: You can select a page number, line number, section number, graphic, table, heading, and many more items from your *Microsoft Word* document.

Bookmarks

A bookmark lets you assign a name to different parts of your document so that you can find that part easily no matter how long the document becomes. A good example is a bookmark for the index in a book. As the book is written, the document gets longer and longer. The writer may want to be able to find the index instantly without scrolling through the document. A bookmark can be used to name almost anything in *Microsoft Word* including graphics, charts, and tables.

Try This:

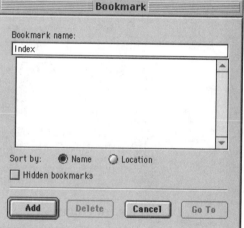

- To add a bookmark, go to the area of the document that you wish to bookmark, and click **INSERT** from the menu bar.

- Select the ***Bookmark*** option from the menu. The **Bookmark** dialog box appears.

- Type the name you wish to call the bookmark, *(Index)*, in the **Bookmark name:** box.

- Click the **Add** button with your mouse button (Macintosh) or left mouse button (Windows). You now have a bookmark named *Index*.

- To check to see what bookmarks you have, click **INSERT** and then *Bookmark*. Is (Index) now on the list?

- To go to a bookmark, select the bookmark that you wish to visit.

- Click the **Go To** button.

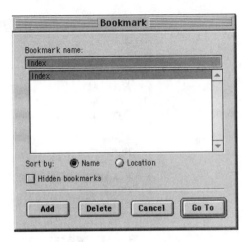

Tips for Success:

If you would like to see where your bookmarks are located in the document, you will have to tell *Microsoft Word* to show them to you.

- To do this, select *Options* (Windows) or *Preferences* (Macintosh) from the **TOOLS** drop down menu. The **Options** or **Preferences** dialog box will appear.

- Point and click in the box to the left of **Bookmarks** under the **View** tab.

- Click the **OK** button.

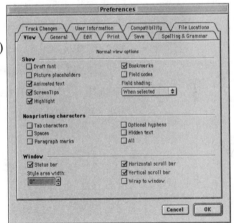

Bookmark
Symbol

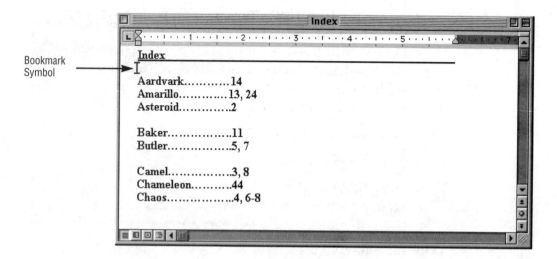

After you have completed a document, you may have little use for
the bookmarks you needed during the creation of the document.

Try This:

- To delete a bookmark, choose *Bookmark* from the **INSERT**
  menu.
- Select the bookmark you wish to delete.
- Click the **Delete** button or press the **Delete** key on your
  keyboard.

Activity #6: Traveling Around

As with each of the skills learned in this book, the more you experiment and practice these skills, the easier and more automatic they will become to you. Here is an activity you can use to practice a little moving around.

1. Open the file (Moving.doc) on your CD-ROM.
2. Press **PageDn** twice.
3. Press **PageUp** once.
4. Press the **Up Arrow** five times.
5. Press the **Down Arrow** four times.
6. Press **Ctrl** (Windows) or ⌘ (Macintosh) and the **Up Arrow**.
7. Press **Ctrl** (Windows) or ⌘ (Macintosh) and **PageDn**.
8. Press **End**.
9. Press the **Left Arrow** six times.
10. Press **Ctrl** (Windows) or ⌘ (Macintosh) and the **Left Arrow** twice.
11. Press **Ctrl** (Windows) or ⌘ (Macintosh) and the **Down Arrow**.
12. Press the **Right Arrow** twice.
13. Press **Home**.
14. Press **PageUp**.
15. Press **Ctrl** (Windows) or ⌘ (Macintosh) and **End**.
16. Press **Home**.
17. Press **Ctrl** (Windows) or ⌘ (Macintosh) and **Home**.

Where did you end up? Right back where you started would be my guess! Using these keys will make working in your projects much easier. Keep practicing and using your skills. Good work!

Find and Replace

Earlier you discovered how to find a word or character in our document using *Microsoft Word*'s **Find** feature. Once you have found that word in your document, you can also ask *Microsoft Word* to replace it with another.

Try This:

- To use **Find and Replace**, select **EDIT** from the menu bar.
- Choose *Replace* from the drop down menu. The **Find and Replace** dialog box will come up with the **Replace** tab selected.

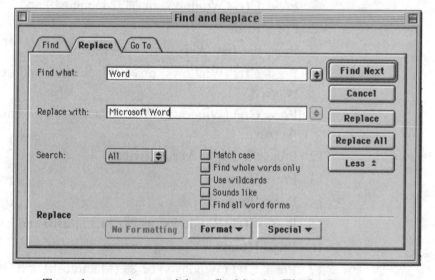

- Type the word you wish to find in the **Find what:** box.
- Type the word you wish to put in its place in the **Replace with:** box.
- Click the **Find Next** button. *Microsoft Word* will search through the document until it finds the next time that the word you have chosen shows up in the document. In this example, it is *(Word)*.

Note: The **Match case** box has been selected so that only (Word) with an initial capital letter will be identified.

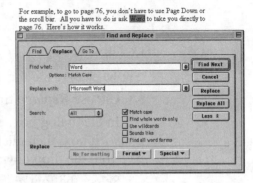

- If you want to replace the word that is now highlighted in your document, click the **Replace** button.
- If you are confident that every occurrence of the word you have entered into the **Find what** box should be replaced, then select **Replace All**.
- After going through the entire document, *Microsoft Word* will tell you when all of the possible changes have been made and give you a count of those changes.
- Click the **Cancel** button to close the **Find and Replace** dialog box.

Tips for Success:

If you are using **Find and Replace** to change an abbreviation into its whole name, be certain the abbreviation cannot be contained within other words. For instance, if you use **Find** to search for the abbreviation RN and wish to replace it with Registered Nurse and do not specify **Match case**, you may find words such as tuRegistered Nurse (formerly turn) and inteRegistered Nurseship (formerly internship). The best safeguard for replacing the correct word is to **Replace** individually instead of using **Replace All**.

Find and Replace can be used to change formatting as well as words.

Try This:

- To change the formatting, select **EDIT** from the menu bar.
- Choose *Replace* from the drop down menu.
- In the dialog box, enter the word to replace in the **Replace with** box, then click the **Format** button, and choose **Font** from the drop down menu.
- Select the font changes and click the **OK** button.

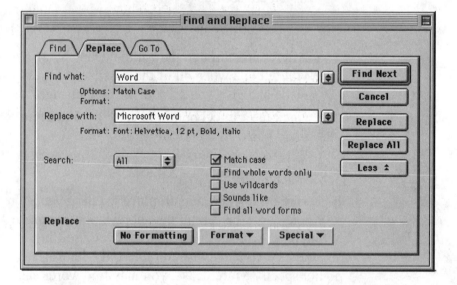

Note: The **Find and Replace** box now has formatting information under the **Replace with** box.

- **Find and Replace** can also find document characters such as: page breaks, tabs, and returns.

Activity #7: Things Just Aren't What They Used to Be!

Find and Replace are powerful features in *Microsoft Word*. They can save you time and frustration if you use them carefully. Take a look.

1. Open the file (Moving.doc) from your CD-ROM.
2. Click *Find* from the **EDIT** menu.
3. Type *(Ctrl)* into the **Find what** box.
4. Click the **Find next** button.
    a. Click the **Find next** button again. Go through the document and find every occurrence of *(Ctrl)*.
    b. Click the **Cancel** button.

Now change all of the *(Ctrl)* to *(Control)*.

1. Click *Replace* from the **EDIT** menu.
2. Type *(Ctrl)* into the **Find what** box.
3. Type *(Control)* into the **Replace with** box.
4. Click the **Find next** button.
5. Click the **Replace** button.
6. If you want to do all of them at once, click the **Replace all** button.
    a. Click the **Cancel** button.

Now scroll through your document and see what you did!

Printing Your Document

Microsoft Word gives you many options to customize the printing of your document.

Try This:

- To print your whole document, click **FILE** from the menu bar.
- Choose *Print* from the drop down menu.

The **Print** dialog box appears (Windows).

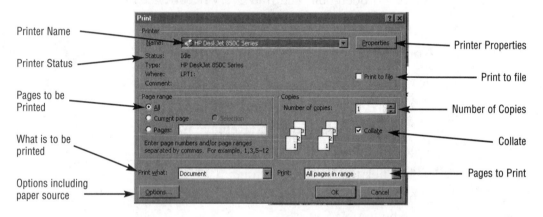

Printer Name → Printer Properties

Printer Status → Print to file

Pages to be Printed → Number of Copies

What is to be printed → Collate

Options including paper source → Pages to Print

The **Print** dialog box appears (Macintosh).

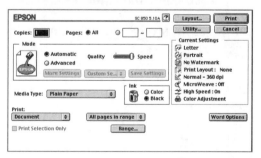

When using a Macintosh platform, the dialog box will differ according to the printer you are using. The information contained in the dialog box will be basically the same. The example used is for an Epson 850 printer.

(Windows) **Printer Name:** refers to the printer you have selected from the printer drivers that have been installed on your computer. Click the right arrow on the **Name:** box. From this list you can click or select the printer where you wish to have your document printed.

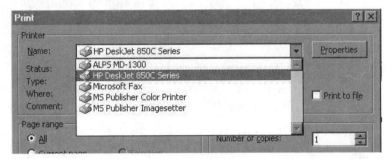

(Macintosh) To choose the printer where you wish to print, select **Chooser** from the **Apple** drop down menu. All of the printer drivers that have been installed on your computer will be listed here. Click the icon of the printer where you wish to have your document printed.

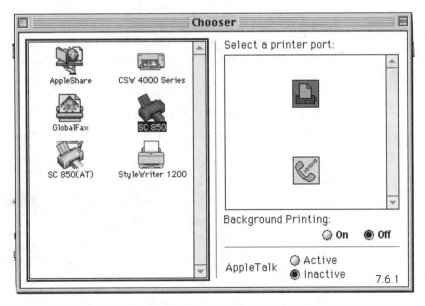

The **Properties** button (Windows) or the ***Print Setup*** option from the **FILE** drop down menu (Macintosh) allows you to select various options available on your printer.

Printer Status tells you what the printer is currently doing. It will tell you where the printer is connected and if it is currently printing or idle. This is a very handy feature if the printer is not next to your computer.

Print to file gives you the option of saving your printed file to the hard drive or a diskette. The file will be saved with a .PRN extension.

The **Page range** box lets you decide what pages you want printed at this time. You have a choice of **All, Current page, Pages** (you can select one or a range of pages), and **Selection**.

Try This:

- To print using **Selection**, select a block of text.
- Click the radio button for **Selection**.
- Click the **OK** button.

Number of Copies is precisely that. How many copies of the document do you want to print?

Collate gives you the option of having your printer collate the document as it prints. Normally, if you requested three copies of a four page document, you would receive four copies of page 1, followed by four copies of page 2, followed by four copies of page 3, and so on. With **Collate** selected, your print request will print page 1, page 2, page 3, then page 4, four times.

Print what lets you select what version of the document you wish to print. Here is the **Print what** dialog box.

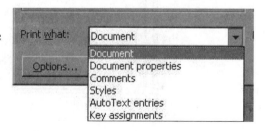

The **Options** box gives you many printing options. Most of these you will never need to change, with one exception. This is the menu where you can choose whether you want to have your paper automatically or manually fed into the printer. You would manually feed transparencies, letterhead, or specialty paper. This option is called the **Default** tray and allows you to choose from **Manual feed** or **Paper Input Bin**.

This option can also be changed in the **Printer Properties** box. **Use printer settings** will use the information from the **Printer Properties** box, if you have not selected one of the other choices here.

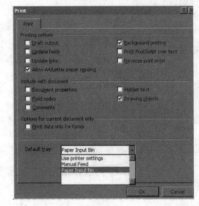

The last option in the **Print** dialog box is **Pages to print**. This allows you to select whether you want to print the entire document, odd pages, or even pages.

Tips for Success:

If you choose to print your document by clicking the **Print** button on the toolbar, your document will print automatically without displaying the **Print** dialog box (Windows). Some print drivers will show the dialog box even if you use the **Print** button on the toolbar (Macintosh).

Canceling a Print Request

You can cancel almost any request in *Microsoft Word* by clicking the **Cancel** button if it is available. The same is true for the print option. After you have clicked the **OK** button at the bottom of the **Print** dialog box, you have several ways to attempt to cancel printing.

Note: These will only work if you cancel before the document is sent to the printer's memory—otherwise know as its buffer.

- (Windows) To cancel your print job, right click the printer icon at the bottom of your Windows screen.

- Left-click **Open Active Printers**.

- Click the document you wish to delete, and press the **Delete** key. This is a very slow process and may or may not be successful. Refer to your printer manual for additional help.

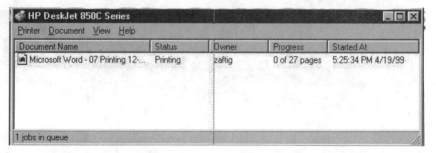

- (Macintosh) To cancel printing, press the **Esc** key on your keyboard or the ⌘ + period(.).

Print Preview

Now that you have done all that work, and your project is entered into the computer, you are curious as to how it will look on the printed page. *Microsoft Word* will let you look at the layout of your document before you send it to the printer.

Try This:

- To preview your document before printing, click **FILE** from the menu bar.
- Choose *Print Preview* from the drop down menu. Your printed page will look exactly as it is presented in the **Print Preview** window.

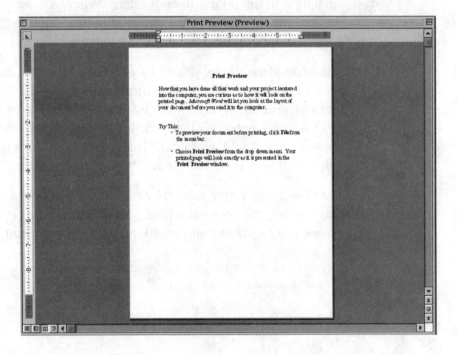

Print Preview gives you several useful tools in its toolbar.

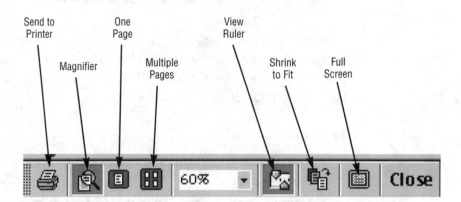

The **Send to Printer** option does precisely that—it sends your document to the printer to be printed. When you press this button, the document bypasses the **Print** dialog box, and you will not be given the opportunity to change any options prior to printing.

The **Magnifier** allows you to zoom in on part of the document to get a closer look. When this button is activated, the cursor looks like a small magnifying glass. Inside the circle is a (+) or a (-). If a (+) shows when you click your left mouse button, the view of your document will get larger. If a (-) shows, a click of the mouse will return your document to its **Print Preview** size.

The **One Page** button tells *Microsoft Word* that you want to preview only one page at a time. The **Multiple Pages** button allows you to see as many as six pages on your screen at one time.

Try This:

- Select *Print Preview* from the **FILE** drop down menu.
- Click the **Multiple Page** button.
- When the drop box appears, highlight the number of pages that you want to see on your screen at one time. When you release the mouse button, the view will change to the number of pages that you have selected.

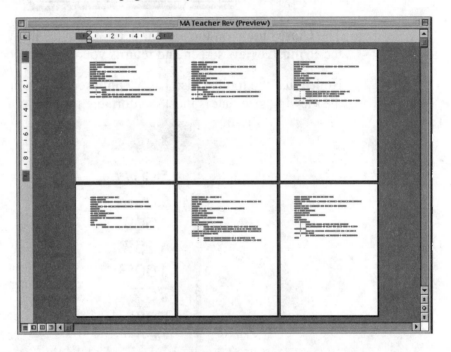

View Ruler allows you to see the ruler above the document. You can make adjustments on this ruler and can see the changes in your document immediately.

With **Shrink to Fit**, *Microsoft Word* attempts to take the entire document and fit it onto one page. If the document is slightly larger than one page, *Microsoft Word* will fit the document on one page in a readable format. If the document is too large, it will make an attempt, but will notify you that after repeated tries it was unable to accomplish the task.

The **Full Screen** button takes your preview of the document and fills the entire screen. To return to the standard screen, click the **Close Full Screen** dialog box.

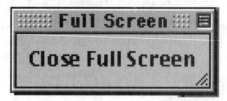

The **Close** button on the toolbar does exactly as it says—it closes the **Print Preview** screen and returns you to your document.

Notice that the toolbar also has a **Zoom** feature. You can choose the viewing size that is most comfortable for you to use.

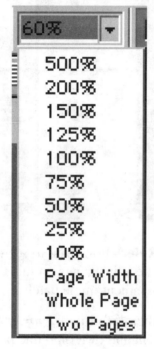

Tips for Success:

Print Preview can save you time, toner, and paper. It can also let you know how your project is proceeding and help you discover when adjustments are needed.

Printing a Specific Page

As you are working on a long document, you will sometimes need to print a specific page. *Microsoft Word* gives you two methods for printing a single, specific page.

Try This:

- To print the page your are currently viewing on your screen, make certain that the I-beam is flashing on the page you want to print.
- Select *Print* from the **FILE** drop down menu. The **Print** dialog box will appear on the screen.

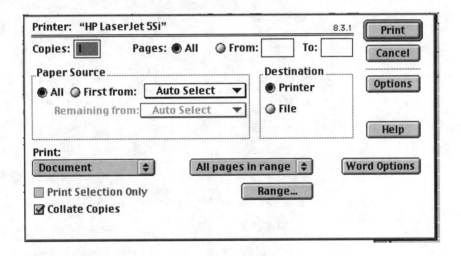

- (Windows) To print the current page only, click **Current page**. (Macintosh) To print current page only, select **Range of pages** and insert the page number into both boxes.
- Click the **OK** button.

Tips for Success:

You can also print a specific page by entering the page number into the **Pages** box. *Microsoft Word* will print only that page.

Printing a Range of Pages

You can print your whole document, or you may wish to print only a few specific pages. Any group of continuous pages within a document is called a range of pages.

Try This:

- To print a range of pages, choose ***Print*** from the **FILE** menu.

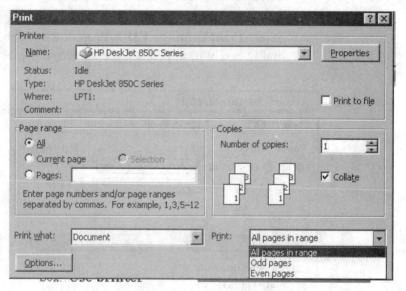

- Enter the range of pages you want printed using a hyphen between the page numbers (Windows). In this example, we have requested pages 8 through 16 to be printed.
- Click the **OK** button.

Tips for Success:

- To print only odd or even pages, choose ***Print*** from the **FILE** menu.
- Click the arrow on the **Print** drop box, and select **Odd Pages**.
- Click the **OK** button.

Printing Several Documents

(Windows only) If you create all of your documents before printing, or use a computer without a printer and need to take it to another location to print, you can send a request to *Microsoft Word* to print all of the documents without going into each document.

Try This:

- To print several documents at the same time, select *Open* from the **FILE** menu.
- Select the documents you wish to print by holding down the **Ctrl** key and clicking the name of each document.
- Click the **Commands and Settings** button.

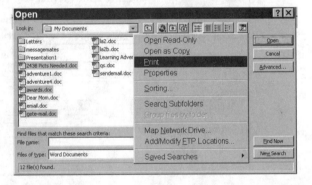

- Click the **Open** button. The documents will be sent to the printer in the order in which they are listed in the Open box.

Tips for Success:

To select consecutive items in the **Open** box, hold down the **Shift** key on your keyboard and click the top and bottom item of the list. All of the items in between will automatically be selected.

To select non-consecutive items, hold down **Ctrl** and click each item you wish to select.

Remember this technique for selecting! You will be using it in several areas of *Microsoft Word*.

Printing More than One Copy

If you need multiple copies of the same document, you will need to tell *Microsoft Word* how many copies you want printed and whether or not you want the pages to be collated.

Try This:

- To print more than one copy, click **FILE** from the menu bar.
- Click the *Print* option from the drop down menu.
- Enter the number of copies you want in the **Number of copies:** box.

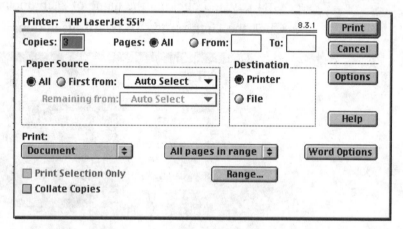

- Select whether or not you want the documents to be **Collated**.
- Click the **OK** button.

Tips for Success:

Be sure to use Print Preview before sending your document to print. This will save you paper and time.

Note: Remember that the print driver software is different for each printer. The dialog boxes may not be exactly like the ones used in this book, but most of them will be similar. You should become familiar with the options your printer offers.

Activity #8: Look What I Did!

You are finally going to get to print out a document. That is why you wanted to learn *Microsoft Word*, isn't it?

1. Open the file *(Note to Parents)* that you created earlier.

2. Click **FILE** on the menu bar.

3. Select *Print Preview*.

How does it look? Does it match what you imagined the finished product to be?

4. Use the **Zoom** to look at the note at 100%.

5. Click the **Close** button.

You can print the note if everything appears to be correct.

6. Click **FILE** on the menu bar.

7. Click *Print*.

8. Select the right printer.

9. Choose how many copies you want of the note.

10. Click **OK**.

There it is! Your first printed document is in your hand. Although you will learn many more things in this book, you now know enough to produce simple letters and notes.

Setting Up and Printing Labels

The office supply store is filled with new types of labels, name tags, and business cards. *Microsoft Word* includes formatting for many of the brand name label products, but you must tell it which label you want to print. It will then format the label automatically.

To set up a label, look at the *Microsoft Word* **Envelopes and Labels** menu.

Try This:

- Start a new document using the **New** icon on your toolbar.

- Click **TOOLS** from the menu bar.
- Select *Envelopes and Labels*. The dialog box for **Envelopes and Labels** will appear.

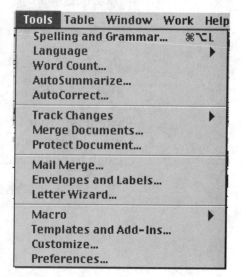

• Select the **Labels** tab.

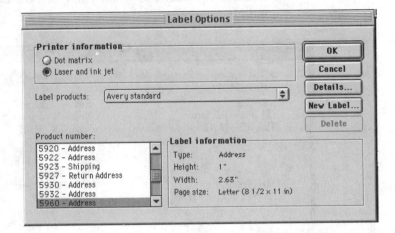

• To choose the style of label you are going to use, click the **Options** button. Select the appropriate label type from the **Label products:** menu and the **Product number:** menu. This number is written on the package containing the labels.

Printer type:
Dot Matrix, Laser
and Ink Jet

Label's name or
brand

Product number

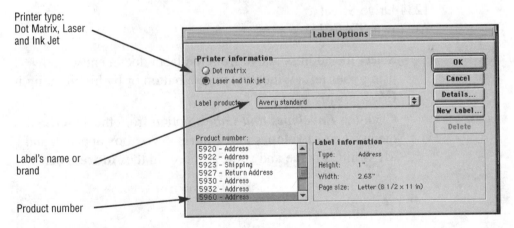

• Click the **OK** button.

• Click the **New Document** button. *Microsoft Word* will start a new formatted sheet where you can enter the names and addresses for each label.

• You can also enter an address into the **Address:** box. When you click the **New Document** button, a formatted sheet of labels with this address will appear.

- You will be given the opportunity to save this label document for later use when you close the document window.

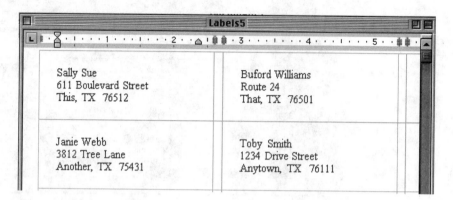

Mr. Smith needs a whole sheet of labels with his name on every label.

Mr. Toby Smith
1234 Drive Street
Anytown, TX 76111

- Select the address above from the label document window using your left (Windows) mouse button or by highlighting it (Macintosh).
- Click the *Envelopes and Labels* option from the **TOOLS** menu. The **Envelopes and Labels** dialog box appears, and Mr. Smith's name and address shows in the **Address** box.

- Click the **Print** button. A sheet of labels with the same address on every label will be printed.

- If you want to print only one label, select the **Single label** button and indicate the number of rows and columns needed.

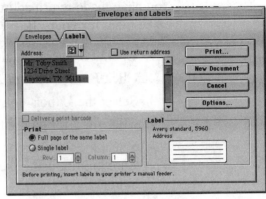

Tips for Success:

If you do a large amount of mailing, you may be able to save a considerable amount of postage expense by placing barcodes on your labels. These barcodes help the U. S. Postal Service automate their system and expedite the delivery of mail.

To turn the barcode feature on so that a barcode will be printed at the bottom of each label, click in the box to the left of **Delivery point barcode**.

The **Labels** feature in *Microsoft Word* can help you create name badges, address labels, business cards, and much more.

Activity #9: Address It Right!

You have made return address labels for Mr. Smith, now you can make them for yourself.

1. Click **TOOLS** from the menu bar.
2. Click ***Envelopes and Labels***.
3. Select the **Labels** tab.
4. Click the **Full page of the same label** button.
5. Select the **Options** button, and choose the label type you want to print using the label product number. Click the **OK** button.
6. Type your return address information into the **Address label** box.
7. Click the **Print** button.

You now have a set of return address labels for your personal use.

Printing Envelopes

Printing envelopes is a snap with *Microsoft Word*. After typing your letter, *Microsoft Word* will locate the address inside of your letter and place it in the proper position on the envelope.

Try This:

- To address an envelope to Mr. Toby Smith, open the letter to Mr. Smith (Smith.doc) from the CD-ROM.
- Select *Envelopes and Labels* from the **TOOLS** drop down menu.
- Choose the **Envelopes** tab. The **Envelope** dialog box appears.

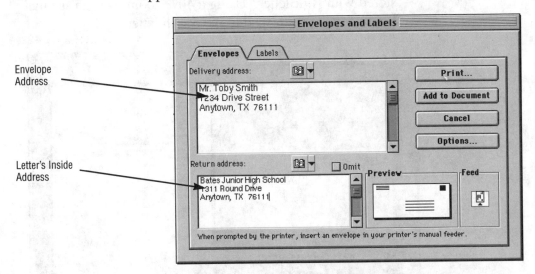

- You can choose to include or not to include your Return address on the envelope. If you have pre-printed envelopes or simply do not want your return address to be printed, point and click in the box to the left of **Omit** and your return address will not be printed.

Tips for Success:

- Click the **Options** button to:

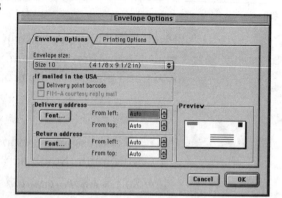

  1. Change the size of the envelope.

  2. Add bar coding to the delivery address.

  3. Format the addresses.

- Click the **Add to Document** button and the envelope will be stored with your letter. Using a 40% zoom, we can see the Smith envelope attached to the Smith letter.

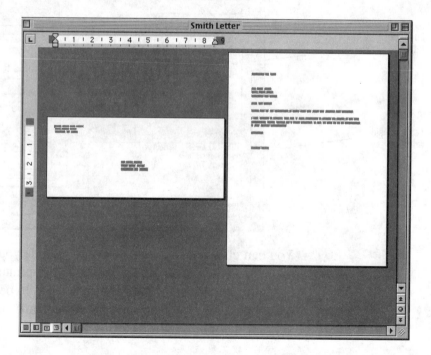

Activity #10: The Envelope, Please!

Envelopes are simple and easy to print using *Microsoft Word*. In this activity, you will address and print an envelope for Mr. Smith. Remember you can print a separate envelope at any time. Even if you are in the middle of another document.

1. Open the *(Smith Letter)* file. *Microsoft Word* will get Mr. Smith's address from the letter.
2. Choose **TOOLS** from the menu bar.
3. Select *Envelopes and Labels* from the drop down menu.
4. Click the **Envelopes** tab.
5. Insert your return address.
6. Click **Options** and select the size envelope you want to use.
7. Place an envelope in your printer. Be sure to check your printer manual to become familiar with the way to load envelopes.
8. Click the **Print** button.

See an example on the CD-ROM (113act10.doc).

Page Setup

Microsoft Word gives you an opportunity to set up the way your document will look by using its Page Setup feature. Some of this section will be different for Windows and Macintosh, and the dialog boxes will vary with different printers, but most of the options will be available to you. Check with your specific printer manual if you can not find a feature mentioned here. The graphics are for a Hewlett Packard printer in a Windows environment.

Through Page Setup, you will be able to:

- Set margins.
- Set position for headers and footers.
- Set paper size.
- Tell *Microsoft Word* if your document will be Portrait or Landscape orientation.
- Set paper source.
- Set other layout options.

By doing a little planning and spending time to set up the document properly initially, you can make your project more manageable and successful. If you have an idea of how you want the project to look before you start, and it has that appearance when it is complete, your feeling of accomplishment will be much greater.

If you do not have the document fully set up when you start or decide to modify it later on, *Microsoft Word* will help.

Try This:

- To access the **Page Setup** dialog box, click **FILE** from the menu bar.
- Click *Page Setup* and the dialog box will open.

Under the **Margins** tab:

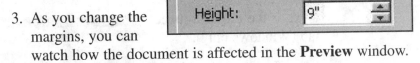

1. You can set the margins for your document.

2. You can set the location of the **Headers** and **Footers**.

3. As you change the margins, you can watch how the document is affected in the **Preview** window.

4. In the **Apply to:** box, *Microsoft Word* gives you the opportunity to make margin changes in **This section**, **This point** forward, **Whole document**.

5. After making changes, click the **OK** button, and your document will be changed.

Another tab or button is **Paper Size:**

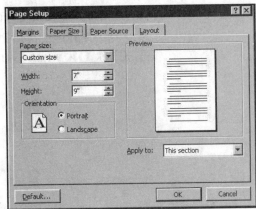

1. Here you can select letter size (8½ x 11), legal size (8½ x 14), or other standard paper sizes.

2. You can decide to design your own paper size by inputting the **Width** and **Height** measurements. When you put in special sizes, the Paper size will read **Custom Size**.

3. You have the option of selecting **Portrait** or **Landscape Orientation** for your document. **Portrait Orientation** is 8½ inches wide by 11 inches tall for a letter size piece of paper. Landscape Orientation is letter size paper sideways or 11 inches wide and 8½ inches tall.

4. Again, you have a choice to apply changes to: **This section, This point forward, Whole document**.

5. Once again, you can preview the changes you make before clicking the **OK** button.

Next, is the **Paper Source** tab (Windows only):

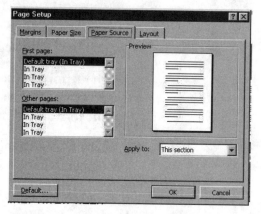

1. Here you can select whether the paper should come from the printer tray or be manually fed. Transparencies and specialty paper often need to be fed manually.

2. To use **Manual Feed**, the printer will pause and ask you to insert a piece of paper before each page that it prints.

3. Click **OK** when you are through making your selections.

Under the Layout tab:

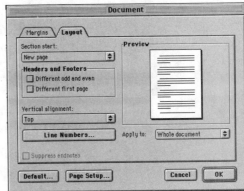

1. You can click the box next to **Line Numbers** to have *Microsoft Word* number every line in your document. Line Numbers are used in legal documents, editing, and poetry as reference points.

2. Select **Line Numbers** to see the dialog box.

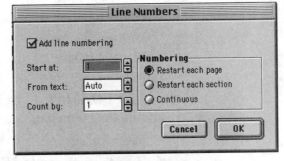

3. Click the **Add line numbering** box. You have the choice of continuous numbering or restarting at the top of each page.

4. Click **OK** to apply line numbers to your document. Here is a sample document with line numbers applied.

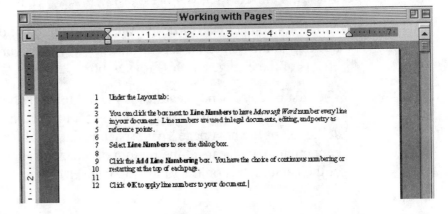

Page Breaks

Microsoft Word can make many decisions for you about starting a new page. It allows you to set some guidelines to follow in determining when to start a new page. *Microsoft Word* will also let you override any of these guidelines and force a page break.

Try This:

- To set these guidelines for text flow, select the paragraphs where you want to control the page break decision.

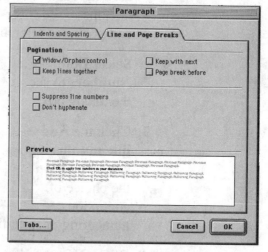

- Click **FORMAT** from the menu bar.
- Select *Paragraph*.
- Click the **Line and Page Breaks** tab.

Each of the six pagination options has a special function in *Microsoft Word*.

Note: As you activate or deactivate any of these options by clicking in the box to the left of the option, you can preview the effects of the changes in the Preview box.

The first of these handy features is the **Widow/Orphan** control. In typesetting, a widow is the last line of a paragraph that ends up at the top of the next page. An orphan is the first line of a paragraph that appears at the bottom of a page when the remainder of the paragraph is on the following page.

The next pagination helper is **Keep Lines Together**. Just as it indicates, this will keep a paragraph all on one page. This sounds like a really great idea, but if you write long paragraphs, you can end up with really empty pages. To have pages with similar amounts of material, divide paragraphs between pages if needed.

Keep with Next will keep a paragraph with the heading that precedes it. This is a handy tool for connecting the two and insuring that the heading does not end up at the bottom of one page while its associated paragraph is on the next page. This should only be used to format a heading and a paragraph and should not be used in the body of the text.

Page Break Before tells *Microsoft Word* to start a new page before the paragraph, which allows you to insure that new topics start on a new page.

Suppress Line Numbers does precisely that. If you have line numbering activated, this command will suppress the numbers in the selected paragraph.

Microsoft Word will automatically make decisions on when to end a line and hyphenate words when the automatic hyphenation is turned on. **Don't hyphenate** allows you to turn off hyphenation for one paragraph.

After selecting the special pagination formatting for your document, click the **OK** button to apply it to the selected paragraphs.

Activity #11: Page Perfect

Now that you have learned about different ways to setup up your page in *Microsoft Word*, you can practice a little.

1. Open the letter to Mr. Smith *(Smith Letter)*.

2. Click **FILE** and choose *Page Setup*.

3. Click the **Paper Size** tab.

4. Change the paper size to **Executive**.

Look at the changes in the **Preview** window.

5. Change the **Orientation** to **Landscape**.

6. Change it back to **Portrait**.

7. Change the left margin to 1.75".

8. Click **Gutter** to see the changes applied in the **Preview** window.

9. Click **OK**.

Wow! You are really getting good at *Microsoft Word*. On to Headers and Footers.

Headers and Footers

Headers and Footers can be at the top and bottom of every page of a document. They are used to show continuity and convey information. Headers may display chapter titles and topic names. Footers can contain page numbers, dates, and names of books. The information contained in headers and footers must be in the required format or the writer's preference.

On this document, *Working with Pages* is the header. The footer is *Microsoft Word for Terrified Teachers,* the page number, and *Teacher Created Materials, Inc.*

Try This:

- To put a Header and Footer on your document, click **VIEW**.
- Choose *Header and Footer*.

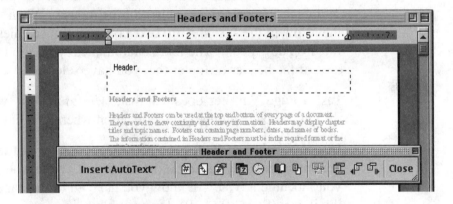

You will see the Header and Footer boxes, but the remainder of the text on the sheet will be 'grayed-out.'

The **Header and Footer** menu bar contains several very helpful tools to assist you in setting up your page.

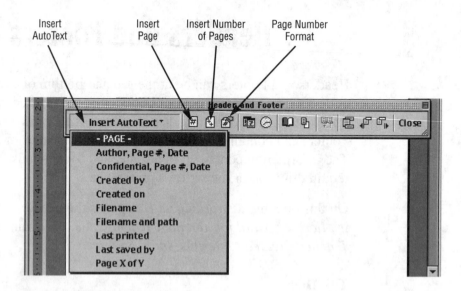

Several pieces of information are commonly used in Headers and Footers. **Insert AutoText** allows you to insert this information into your document with a click of the mouse. When you click the arrow in the **Insert AutoText** box, you can see these items in the drop down box. The text is automatically inserted into the area of the header or footer that you have selected.

Insert Page Number does just that. *Microsoft Word* will insert the current page number in the location where you have selected.

Insert Number of Pages is a convenient feature that tells you how many total pages are in the document. Now when you print your document, you will know you have all of the pages because it will say (Page 10 of 10), for example.

The **Format Page Number** button allows you to change how the numbers are presented in your document. When you select the **Format Page Number** button, a dialog box appears with several choices.

Number format allows you to select:

1, 2, 3, . . .

A, B, C, . . .

a, b, c, . . .

i, ii, iii, . . .

I, II, III, . . .

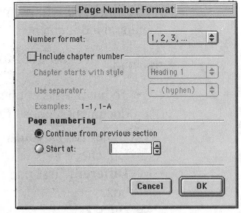

You can also choose to **Include chapter number** if your document is set up with chapter numbers.

Page Number Format gives you the option of numbering your documents continuously from one to the last page, or you can type a page number in the **Start at** box. Use this option if you are printing a section of a much longer document.

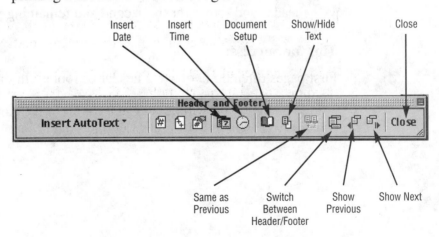

Insert Date and **Insert Time** are self-explanatory.

The **Switch Between Header and Footer** button lets you alternate between viewing the header and viewing the footer in your document.

Microsoft Word will permit you to put different headers and footers in a document.

Try This:

- To put a different header and footer on the first page of your document, choose *Page Setup* from the **FILE** menu.
- Under the **Layout** tab, check the **Different first page** box.
- Click **OK**.
- Go to the first page of your document and set up the header and footer for the first page only.

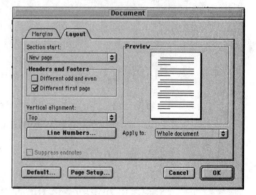

- Go to the second page of your document and set up the header and footer for the second and remaining pages.

Tips for Success:

First pages often do not have a header or footer. In that case, you would leave them blank.

Many times a magazine will put one footer, such as the magazine's name, on the even pages, and another footer, such as the date of the issue, on the odd pages. This is accomplished by selecting the **Different odd and even** box and putting a different footer on the odd and even pages.

Try This:

- To set up a different header and footer for odd and even pages, click **Different odd and even** from the **Page Setup** dialog box.
- Click **OK**.
- Front pages and title pages often do not have headers or footers. In this instance, you would click on **Different first page** and leave the header and footer blank.
- Go to page 3 to set up the header and footer for the odd pages.
- Go to page 2 to set up the header and footer for the even pages.

Another time where you would want to have a different header and footer in your document could be when the document is composed of different sections. You will learn about that next.

Section Breaks

To use different formatting from one part of your document to the next, you will need to insert section breaks. Specifically, if you want to have different headers and footers, to change margins, to insert columns, or to add other major formatting, you will need to divide your document into different parts. Though the document will still all be together in the same file, the different sections will carry significantly different formatting.

Try This:

- To insert a section break, click **INSERT**.
- Choose *Break*, and a dialog box will appear.
- Select the type of **Section Break** you want to insert.

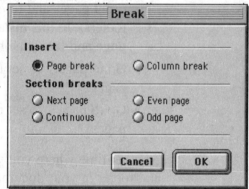

Next page inserts a section break on a new page.

Continuous inserts a section break on the current page.

Even page inserts a section break on a new even page.

Odd page inserts a section break on a new odd page.

- Click **OK** to insert the break. The break will be inserted where your insertion point is blinking or there after.

The following is an example of a continuous section break inserted into a document. Notice that you must be in the **Normal View** to see the section break.

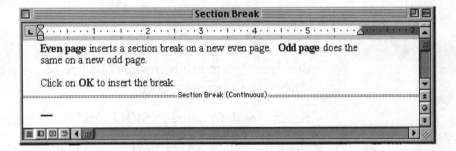

Even page inserts a section break on a new even page. **Odd page** does the same on a new odd page.

Click on **OK** to insert the break.

Try This:

- To delete the section break, go to the **Normal View**.
- Click directly under the **Section Break** line.
- Press the **Backspace** (Windows) or **Delete** (Macintosh) key.
- Then press **Delete** (Windows) or **Del** (Macintosh) key.

Once the section break is deleted, the text will be formatted in the same manner as the text above the section break.

Section breaks are needed to change the headers and footers from one section of the document to another. For example, when the name of the chapter appears in the header. Once the chapter changes, so must the header.

Try This:

- To change the header and footer in the middle of a document, go to just below the last line of the section before where the change is needed.

- Select *Break* from the **INSERT** drop down menu.

- Click the button beside **Next page** and then click **OK**. A section break has now been inserted.

- Place the I-beam after the section break.

- Select *Header and Footer* from the **VIEW** menu.

- Click in the header box to be changed.

- From the **Header and Footer** toolbar, press the **Same as previous** button to deactivate this command. This causes the previous section's information to be discontinued in the new section.

- Now you are free to put the new information into the header and footer and that information will carry forward until you enter a new section break or to the end of the document.

Two other buttons are available on your **Header and Footer** toolbar that can help you in organizing your document. These buttons are the **Show Next** and **Show Previous** buttons.

These buttons let you move between the previous section's header and footer to the next section's header and footer.

The last button on the **Header and Footer** toolbar is the **Switch Between Header and Footer** button, and allows you to do just that.

Press this button to jump from header to footer without scrolling through the entire page.

Tips for Success:

Using headers and footers will help the reader navigate his way through your document.

Page Numbers

As we saw in the section on headers and footers, page numbers are easily inserted into *Microsoft Word* documents. In addition to going through **Insert Page Numbers** on the **Header and Footer** menu bar, you can also use the **INSERT** menu.

Try This:

- To insert page numbers into your document, click the **INSERT** menu.
- Click *Page Numbers*, and the **Page Numbers** dialog box appears.

The **Position** box lets you select whether you want the page number to be at the top or bottom of the page.

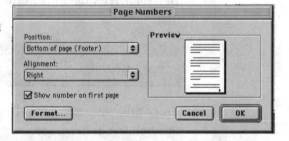

The **Alignment** box lets you select how you want the number to be aligned: right, left, center, or outside.

You can also click the **Show number on first page** box to tell *Microsoft Word* if you want a page number to appear on the first page of your document.

Tips for Success:

As you make selections in the **Page Numbers** box, you can preview your decision. **Format** lets you change the way your page numbers are presented as discussed earlier in this section.

Activity #12: From Top to Bottom

Notice the header and footer on this page. They make it nice when you are trying to find where you are and what you are studying. Now you will add headers and footers to the file (Moving.doc).

1. Open the file (Moving.doc) from the CD-ROM.

2. Click **VIEW** and choose *Header and Footer*.

3. Click in the **Header** box and type *(Arrow, Home, & End Keys)*.

4. Click the **Switch Between Header and Footer** button in the toolbar.

5. Click in the **Footer** box.

6. Click the **Insert Page Number** button.

7. Space and type *(of)* and space again.

8. Click the **Number of Pages** button.

9. Space and type *(Pages)*.

10. Use the **Zoom** box on your menu bar to look at your document. To see both pages at once, click two pages.

Font Style

Earlier, we discussed all of the different fonts that are available in *Microsoft Word*. Now we will take a look at the fun things you can do with the fonts.

First we have those font styles that are used all of the time in almost every document: bold, italics, and underline. These are used so often that *Microsoft Word* has included them in the Standard toolbar.

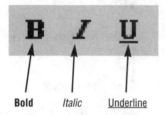

Bold   *Italic*   <u>Underline</u>

You can click these buttons prior to typing a word or select the word or words, and then press the button.

You can combine these buttons to expand your choice of effects.

Bold Italic

<u>Bold Italic Underline</u>

<u>Italic Underline</u>

Plain Text

Microsoft Word has even more effects in its **Font** dialog box.

- Click **FORMAT** from the menu bar.
- Select *Font* from the drop down menu. A dialog box will appear.

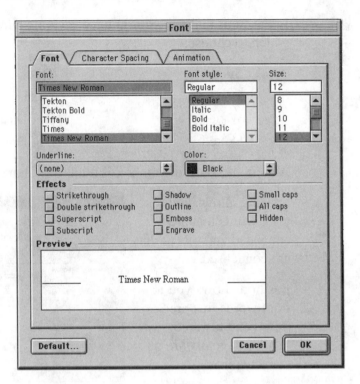

Try some of these examples of the different effects, and view them in the **Preview** box.

~~Strikethrough~~

Superscript

Subscript

Shadow

Outline

Emboss

Engrave

SMALL CAPS

ALL CAPS

Now try a couple of the combinations.

Shadow Outline

In the **Font** dialog box, you have several styles of underlines from which to choose:

Single	Thick
Double	Dash
Wave	Dot Dash
Dotted	Dot Dot Dash

Also in the **Font** dialog box is a tab for **Character Spacing**.

Spacing allows you to print words that are expanded and others that are condensed.

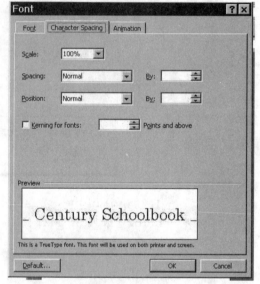

Position allows you to print words that are raised and lowered. Yes, these really are on the same line!

Animation is also available through *Microsoft Word* in the Animation tab in the **Font** dialog box. You can explore this on your own, because the printed page just does not do it justice.

Another thing that is impossible to show you in a black and white printed book is *Microsoft Word*'s ability to use different colored text. Click the **Color** drop box in the **Font** dialog box.

Just imagine all of these great colors! You can change the color of your font on the screen, and if you have a color printer, the colors you have selected will show on your printed page as well.

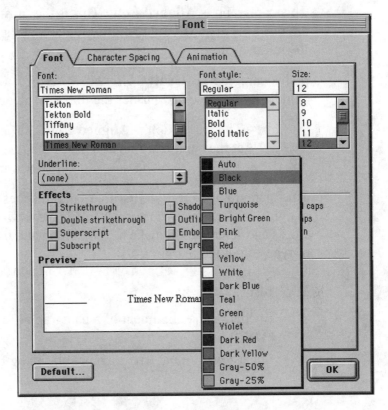

You can select the color of your choice from your toolbar also. You can really enjoy experimenting with all of these font styles and colors!

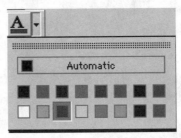

Alignment

You can use the **Alignment** or **Justification** feature of *Microsoft Word* to enhance the appearance of your documents. You have four different ways that you can justify your paragraphs.

This paragraph is **Aligned Left**. This is the most common alignment format. Every line of type starts at the same place on the left margin.

This paragraph is **Center Aligned**. *Microsoft Word* starts in the middle of the page and pushes the line of type out to each margin.

This paragraph is **Aligned Right**. *Microsoft Word* starts at the right margin and pushes the line of type backward toward the left margin.

This paragraph is fully **Justified** and reaches from margin to margin. Notice that *Microsoft Word* leaves extra spaces between words and sentences to make the beginning and the end of each line of type end at the margin.

Try This:

- To change the alignment of a paragraph or document, click **FORMAT**.
- Select *Paragraph*. The **Paragraph** dialog box will appear.

- Choose the **Indents and Spacing** tab.
- Click the arrow in the **Alignment** box.
- Select the alignment you wish to use.
- Click **OK**.

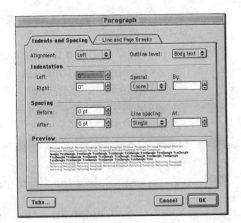

Tips for Success:

- You can also align text using your toolbar.

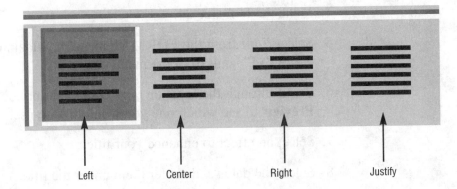

| Left | Center | Right | Justify |

- Alignment can be used to position paragraphs, words, titles, and text within tables.
- Alignment can significantly change how your document appears. Check margins and page breaks after changing the alignment of an entire document.

Activity #13: Document Makeover

Now you are finally getting to the fun stuff. Have you looked through the fonts on your computer? There are so many fun fonts to use and different effects to apply.

You can make that field day note a bit more attractive.

1. Open the file *(Note to Parents)*.

2. Select the first line by clicking in the left margin.

3. Center the title using the **Center Alignment** button on the toolbar.

4. Make the font size 24.

5. Select *Font* from the **FORMAT** menu or (Macintosh) click the **FONT** menu from the menu bar.

6. Scroll through the fonts on your computer and look at the **Preview** to see which one you would like to use.

7. Select an effect to enhance your title.

8. Select the dates and center them under the title.

9. Select *(See you on the 6th)*.

10. **Bold** and **Underline** the sentence.

Your note definitely looks better. Your students' parents will surely notice this note!

See an example on the CD-ROM (138act13.doc).

Formatting Paragraphs and Blocks of Text

Formatting paragraphs or blocks of text is easy to do in *Microsoft Word*. Select the text you want to format and click the appropriate formatting button from the toolbar. We all know what a paragraph is, but what constitutes a block of text? A block of text might be a sentence, several sentences, a paragraph, or several paragraphs. Basically, a block of text is any selection of text that is all together.

Try This:

- To format a block of text, select the block of text to format by double-clicking in the left margin of the first paragraph.
- Click the formatting button on the toolbar that you want to use.

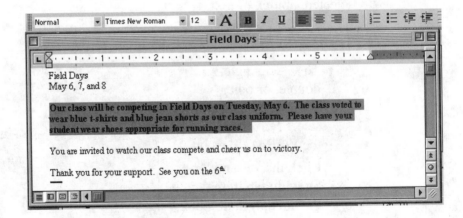

Tips for Success:

While you have the text selected, you can choose multiple formats, such as: bold, italics, and right aligned.

Line Spacing

You can change the appearance of your document by using single-, one-and-a-half-, or double-spacing in your document. You can select single- or double-spacing from your toolbar in some versions of *Microsoft Word*.

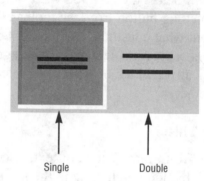

Single   Double

You can change the spacing on a document in two ways. First, before you begin to enter your text, or second, after you have selected a block of text.

Try This:

- To select single, double, or other variations of spacing, select *Paragraph* from the **FORMAT** menu.

- Click the **Indents and Spacing** tab in the **Paragraph** dialog box.

- Click the down arrow in the **Line spacing** box.

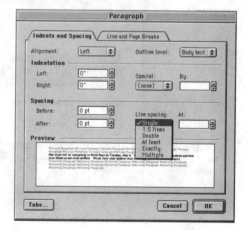

- Select the spacing you would like to use in your document.

Activity #14: Reading Between the Lines

When you are creating a document for other people to read, consistent formatting is extremely important. If the information is complex, white space can aid in comprehension.

1. Open (Moving.doc) from the CD-ROM.

2. Print out a copy of the document.

3. Notice that on the second page, some of the instructions are single-spaced while on the first page they are all double-spaced.

4. Select the first line in each of the single-spaced lists and click the **Double Space** button on your toolbar, or choose *Paragraphs*, then *Indents and Spacing* from the **FORMAT** menu.

The document looks better and is consistent from page to page. Changing the spacing in a document can also affect where the page breaks occur. Click the **Zoom** button on the toolbar and choose the **Two Pages** view to check this document. The page breaks are still fine.

Indentation

Indenting the first line of a paragraph is the same in *Microsoft Word* as it was on the old manual typewriters. When you are ready to indent, press the **Tab** key. Of course, that is not all that *Microsoft Word* allows you to do. You can also do indentations from both sides for quotations and hanging indents for references. It will even indent the first paragraph automatically so that you do not have to press **Tab**.

Try This:

- To indent a paragraph from both the left and right sides of the page, click **FORMAT**.

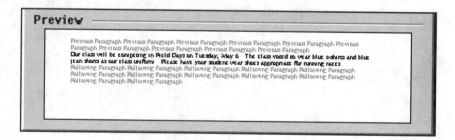

- Select *Paragraph*.
- Change the **Left** and **Right** indentation amounts on the **Indents and Spacing** tab.
- Preview your changes in the **Preview** box.

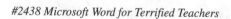

- Click **OK**.

Hanging indents are used in references and bibliographies. As you can see from this paragraph, the first line remains at the left margin while the remaining lines are indented .5 inches.

- From the **Paragraph** dialog box on the **Indents and Spacing** tab, click the down arrow by the Special box.
- Select **Hanging**.
- Click **OK**.

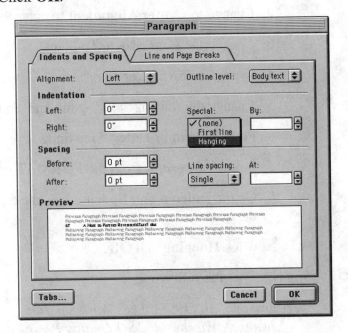

Tips for Success:

If you set your indentation formatting prior to entering text in a document, it will remain in effect until you change the settings back to normal.

You can format a paragraph you have already typed by selecting the paragraph and then choosing *Paragraph* from the **FORMAT** menu.

Activity #15: Take One Step Forward

You are in the habit of using an indentation for the first sentence of a paragraph, but there are other times that indentations can make your documents more readable or follow specific formats. Type this example of a hanging indentation used for a reference in a paper.

1. Open a new document.

2. Change to **Center Alignment** to enter the title.

3. Change the **Font Size** to 16-point.

4. Type *(REFERENCES)*.

5. Change the font size to 12-point and change to **Align Left**.

6. Press **Return** or **Enter** three times.

7. Select *Paragraph* from the **FORMAT** menu.

8. On the **Indents and Spacing** tab, click the **Special** arrow for the drop box.

9. Click **Hanging** and **OK**.

10. Type the following:

(Caravatta, M. (1998). Let's Work Smarter, Not Harder. Milwaukee, Wisconsin: ASQ Quality Press.)

See an example on the CD-ROM (144act15.doc).

Not bad! Now look at more ammunition for enhancing your documents—the bullet.

Bullets and Numbers

Microsoft Word can automatically bullet or number your lists.

- Use the **Bullet** button on your toolbar to make a bulleted list.

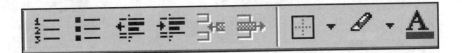

- To number a list, click the **1, 2, 3** button on your toolbar.

Tips for Success:

- To change the look of your bulleted list, click **FORMAT**.
- Select *Bullets and Numbering*.
- Click the **Bulleted** tab.
- Click the style of bullet you wish to use in your document.
- Click the **OK** button.

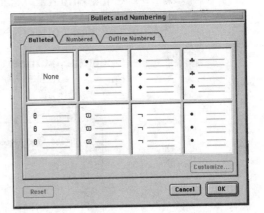

- *Microsoft Word* allows you to change the symbols you use as bullets. Click one of the bullet selections and then click the **Customize** button. The **Customized Bulleted List** dialog box appears.

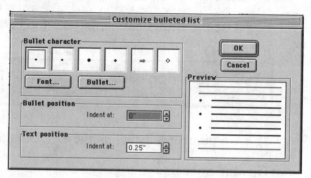

- Click **Bullet** to select a new symbol for use as a bullet.

Microsoft Word offers several selections for numbering as well.

- Under the **Numbered** tab, you can see the choices and select one.

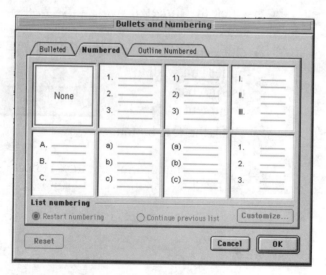

- You also have the choice to **Restart numbering,** restarting the numbers at the beginning of each list, or **Continue previous list**.

Activity #16: Do You Get the Point?

Bullets help important points stand out in your document. Numbers tell the reader the order in which things should be completed or that the writer does not want the reader to miss part of the list. A numbered list lets the reader know if an item is missing, such as in a packing slip.

For this activity, type this list of instructions that you want your students to complete.

(Arrive at school by 8:15 a.m.

Hang up your coat.

Put your books in your locker.

Get your book and notebook for first period.

Get to first class by 8:25 a.m.

Be seated and ready to work.)

1. After typing this list, select all of the lines.

2. Click the **Bullet** button on the toolbar.

3. Select ***Bullets and Numbering*** from the **FORMAT** menu.

4. Click the **Bulleted** tab.

5. Select the square boxes.

6. Click **OK**.

You have just changed the list into a checklist. The box can be checked to show completion of each task.

See an example on the CD-ROM (147act16.doc).

Changing Margins

There are several ways to change margins in *Microsoft Word*. In a new document, set the margins using *Page Setup* from the **FILE** menu.

If you want to change the margins for the whole document after it is entered, use the **Ruler** bar at the top of the **Print Preview** screen.

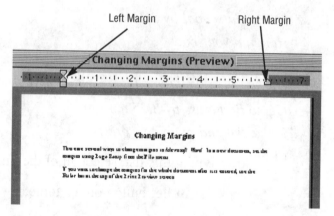

Try This:

- Point and hold down the left mouse button on one of the margins. Drag the pointer to the new location and release the button.
- When you are through changing margins, click **Close** to return to your document.

Tips for Success:

- To change right and left margins for only part of the document, use *Paragraph* from **FORMAT** drop down menu and then the **Indents and Spacing** tab.
- To change top and bottom margins for the entire document, use *Page Setup* from the **FILE** menu.
- To change top and bottom margins for only one page of the document, you will need to insert section breaks.

Changing Tab Settings

When you are typing a document that has columns of information in it, you will want all of the columns to line up evenly to make your document more readable. *Microsoft Word* has four different types of tab settings that you can use: Left, Right, Centered, and Decimal.

Try This:

- To insert a **Tab** into your document before entering text, select the type of Tab you want to insert by clicking the button at the top of your document on the left. It will click through the tab choices.

- Point and click the location where you want the **Tab** to be placed on the **Ruler Bar**. The **Tab** is inserted at that point.

- To insert a **Tab** into a document that you have already entered text into, select the text where you want to insert the **Tab**.

- Select the type of **Tab** you want inserted.

- Point and click the **Ruler Bar** where you want the **Tab** to be located.

- Use your mouse to click in the text where the **Tab** should be inserted.

- Press **Tab** on your keyboard.

Tips for Success:

Always use tabs instead of spaces in your document to line up text. Using tabs insures that your printer knows exactly where you want the words to start.

When you start a new document, *Microsoft Word* sets a tab every 0.5 inches across the page. To change the location of the **Tabs**, point and hold down the left mouse button on the **Tab** button on the **Ruler Bar** and drag the **Tab** to the new location.

You can also set up your **Tabs** to insert leader dots such as in a table of content and index. To format **Tabs** to insert leaders:

- Select *Tabs* from the **FORMAT** menu.

- Insert the **Tab stop position** in the box.

- Select the type of **Leader**.

- Click **OK**.

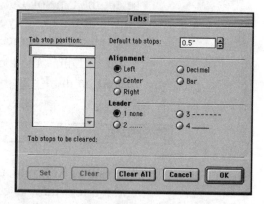

A line using tabs and leaders dots will look like this:

Using Columns

The column feature is an easy way to layout newsletters and flyers. You can type in a column of text and *Microsoft Word* will format it automatically. As you type, the words will go from the top to the bottom margin and then return to the top of the next column.

Try This:

- To start columns in your document, click the **Columns** button on your toolbar.

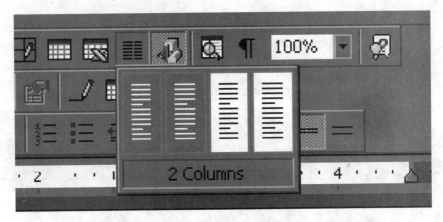

- Point at the drop down box and hold down the left mouse button until you have colored in the number of columns you want in your document. Release the mouse button. The Columns feature has now been activated.

Tips for Success:

To format text into columns that you have already entered:

- Select the text.
- Click the **Columns** button on the toolbar.
- Select the number of columns by holding down the mouse button.

To remove the columns formatting from your document:

- Select the text to be reformatted.
- Click the **Columns** button on the toolbar.
- Click the first column only.

You can also choose *Columns* from the **FORMAT** menu to insert column formatting into your document. You will have a wider range of choices from this dialog box, and you can also preview how the choices you have made will look.

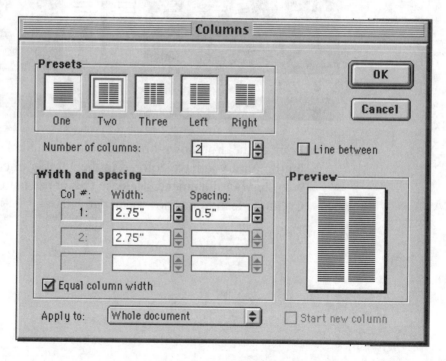

Microsoft Word Has Done the Work

Many documents are created repeatedly that have special formatting or need to have a certain appearance. *Microsoft Word* has several of these special documents ready for your use. The special tools used for this are called **Wizards** and **Templates**, and you just fill in the blanks or answer the questions.

A **Template** is a form that you open on your screen, and you simply customize it to suit your needs.

A **Wizard** asks you a series of questions and then uses your responses to help you prepare the document.

Try This:

- To start a **Wizard** or **Template**, click **FILE**.
- Click *New*.
- Click the **Letters & Faxes** tab. Under the **Letters & Faxes** tab are several choices. The Wizards have the word *Wizard* in their description.

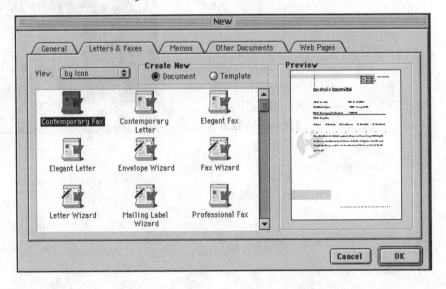

- To look at a template first, double-click the **Contemporary Fax** icon.

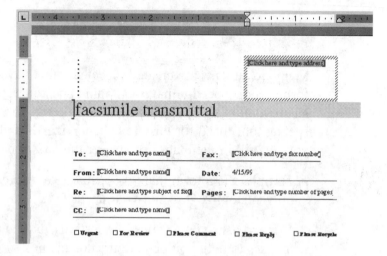

facsimile transmittal

To:	[Click here and type name]	Fax:	[Click here and type fax number]
From:	[Click here and type name]	Date:	4/15/99
Re:	[Click here and type subject of fax]	Pages:	[Click here and type number of pages]
CC:	[Click here and type name]		

□ Urgent   □ For Review   □ Please Comment   □ Please Reply   □ Please Recycle

Notice that the template says *[Click here and type . . .]* at each place where you need to supply information. This gives you a quick, easy way to fill out standard documents that you do not create yourself, and it looks professional and personalized.

Try This:

- To look at a wizard, once again, click **FILE**.
- Click *New*.
- This time look under the **Memos** tab and double-click the **Memo Wizard** icon.

The **Memo Wizard** will walk you through creating a memo, letting you choose wording, styles, and formats.

Simply read each of the questions that the wizard asks and fill in any information requested. Click **Next** after you have completed each screen. If you want to make a change, click **Back** and make the changes. After you have answered all of the wizard's questions, click **Finish** and your memo form will be set up and ready to go. The last step is to write your memo!

Tips for Success:

In *Microsoft Word*, you will find Wizards to make:

- Letters
- Faxes
- Memos
- Envelopes
- Mailing Labels
- Résumés

You can also go to the Internet and get additional wizards at the *Microsoft Word* Web site.

Activity #17: Elegant Letter

This activity lets you practice using one of *Microsoft Word*'s built-in templates.

1. Select *New* from the **FILE** menu.
2. Click the **Letters & Faxes** tab.
3. Double-click the **Elegant Letter** icon.

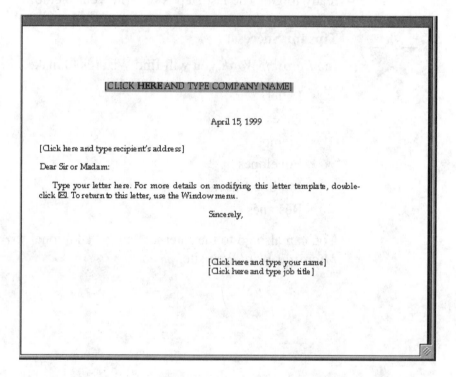

Click each area of the template and fill in your information. Do not forget the **Header and Footer** on this template. These areas customize your document and make them look more professional.

See an example on the CD-ROM (156act17.doc).

Activity #18: Fax Wizard

The **Fax Wizard** will let you set up the standard fax information that you use each time you send a fax.

1. Select **New** from the **FILE** menu.
2. Click the **Letter & Faxes** tab.
3. Double-click the **Fax Wizard** icon.

The Fax Wizard will appear on the screen.

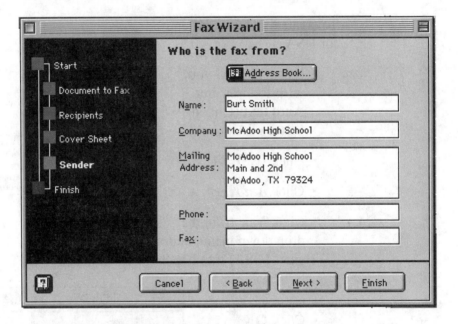

4. Complete the blanks and click **Next**.
5. After entering all of the needed information, click **Finish**.

You can even tell *Microsoft Word* to send the fax if you have your computer configured to use a modem and fax.

See an example on the CD-ROM (157act18.doc).

Creating an AutoText Entry

AutoText is very similar to **AutoCorrect**; it helps you enter common phrases into your documents efficiently and accurately. For example, you can enter the letters "USA" and then have *Microsoft Word* automatically insert the words "United States of America."

Try This:

To create the **AutoText** entry for USA:

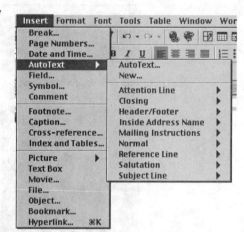

- Select the text you wish to insert into **AutoText** (United States of America).

- Click **INSERT**.

- Click *AutoText*.

- Click *New* from the drop down menu, and enter (USA) into box.

- Click **OK**.

To use your AutoText:

- Click **INSERT**.

- Select *AutoText*.
- Click *Normal* from the drop down menu.
- Click the AutoText name *(USA)*. "United States of America" will be inserted at the insertion point.

To look at the AutoText entries that are automatically entered into *Microsoft Word* and insert them into your document:

- Click **INSERT**.
- Click *AutoText*.
- Click *AutoText* again in the drop down menu.
- When the dialog box appears, use the scroll bar to see a full list of entries.
- Select the entry you want to use.
- Click the **Insert** button to place it into your document.

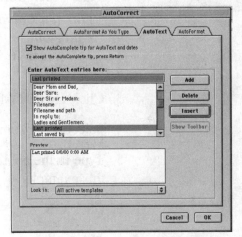

Tips for Success:

Use **Filename** and **Path** from **AutoText** to help you remember where you saved a document.

Activity #19: Saying the Same Ole Thing

Microsoft Word will let you set up your own customized AutoText entries for those phrases that you use on a daily basis. For this activity, you will add an AutoText entry and see how well it works in your document.

1. Type in the following information into a new document. This is the information that AutoText will insert.

   (Tarrant County Junior College
   Office of Continuing Education)

2. Select the text.

3. Click **INSERT** from the menu bar, and select *AutoText*.

4. Select *New* from the next drop down menu.

5. Type in the abbreviation you wish to use—*(TCJOCE)*, for this example.

6. Click **OK**.

Now, to test the entry, type *(TCJOCE)*.

7. Select the abbreviation.

8. Click **INSERT** from the menu bar, select *AutoText*, and then *Normal*.

9. Click TCJOCE and the full phrase will be inserted.

Drawing Tables

Tables give you an opportunity to organize information in your project so that it is clearly understood and neatly presented. *Microsoft Word* assists you in formatting the tables to make them look professional and attractive.

Try This:

- To create a table, click **TABLE** from the menu bar.
- Click *Insert Table*, and the **Insert Table** dialog box appears.

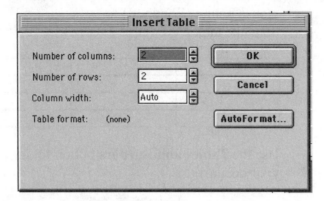

- Insert the number of columns and rows that you want in your table.
- Select **Auto** for **Column** width to let *Microsoft Word* determine the width of your columns or enter an exact size. You can also use the up and down arrows to select a size.
- Click **OK** and the table template will be inserted into your document at the location where your insertion point is blinking.
- Type headings and information into each cell of the table.
- Use the **Tab** key to move from one cell to the next.

Tips for Success:

You can also select the **Insert Table** button from the toolbar. After clicking the button, drag the mouse and highlight the size table that you need. In this example, the highlighted squares fill an area that is 3 rows by 4 columns.

Release the mouse button (Macintosh) or click the left mouse button (Windows) to draw the table.

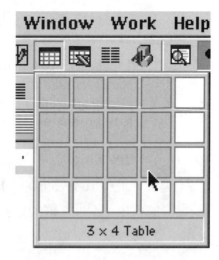

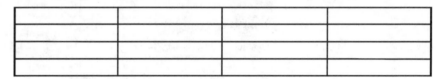

Use the **Tables and Borders** button to draw and format tables in your documents.

The **Tables** and **Borders** button gives you several options for changing the appearance of your table.

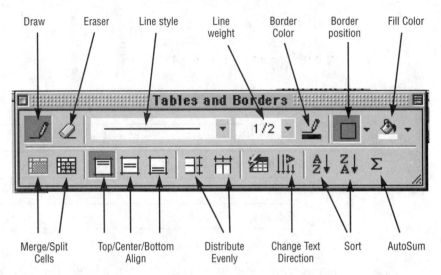

Draw and **Eraser** let you draw lines into your table or erase lines that you do not wish to keep in the table.

Line Style, **Line Weight**, **Border Color**, **Border Position**, and **Fill Color** add to the aesthetics of your table.

Merge Cells and **Split Cells** allow you to make changes in the layout of the table to accommodate titles and variable sized cells.

The **Align** buttons allow you to decide if you want the table to be at the **Top**, the **Bottom**, or in the **Center** of your page.

The **Distribute Evenly** buttons allow you to specify if you want all of the rows or columns to be the same size.

The **Change Text Direction** button allows you to put titles in your table that run vertically, for example:

	Monday	Tuesday	Wednesday	Thursday	Friday
Sunny					
Lisa					
Laura					
Toby					
Rosie					

Sort permits you to sort the rows of a table in either Ascending or Descending order easily. Look at the same table sorted in A to Z order.

	Monday	Tuesday	Wednesday	Thursday	Friday	TOTAL
Laura	5	8	4	3	9	29
Lisa	6	7	9	6	4	29
Rosie	8	4	6	8	5	31
Sunny	7	3	5	8	4	27
Toby	6	4	8	5	7	27

AutoSum will total the amounts entered into the rows or columns of a table automatically. To use AutoSum, click the cell where you want the total to show, and click the AutoSum button.

AutoFormatting Tables

Microsoft Word will assist you in making your tables appear clearer by giving you a choice of different table formats and layouts.

Try This:

- To use AutoFormat while creating a table, click **TABLE**.
- Click *Insert Table*.
- Click *AutoFormat*.

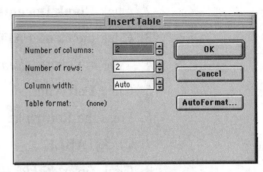

The **Table AutoFormat** dialog box appears.

- Scroll through the **Formats** box and Preview each of the formats available in *Microsoft Word*.
- Click in the boxes to the left of the different **Formats to apply** options and the **Apply special formats to** section.

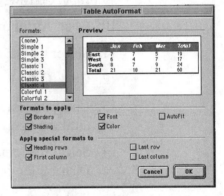

Click **OK** to apply these formats to your new table.

Tips for Success:

To apply a Table Autoformat to an existing table, select the entire table and select *Table AutoFormat* from the **TABLE** menu.

Activity #20: Just Set the Table

Tables can be very useful tools in the classroom. Here is an idea for a reading log form that can easily be set up using the Tables feature.

1. Click *New* in the **FILE** menu.

2. Click **Blank Document**.

3. Click the **Center Aligned** button.

4. Type in the title *(Reading Log)*.

5. Click **Left Aligned**.

6. Press the **Return** key three times.

7. Click **TABLE**.

8. Click *Insert Table*.

9. Input 30 rows and 16 columns.

10. Click **AutoFormat**.

11. Select the format you want to use.

12. Click **OK**.

13. Using the column dividers, move the columns to the right until the first column expands to $1/3$ of the page.

14. Select the remaining columns and click the Even Distribution button.

15. In the first cell, type *(Student's Name)*.

16. In each of the following cells, across the top row, type the numbers 1 through 15.

17. Save your file as *(Reading Log)*.

That is all you have to do. Your form is now ready for you to enter the students' names and the date that they completed each unit in reading.

See an example on the CD-ROM (166act20.doc).

Creating Outlines

Creating an outline can help you gather your ideas together to present a topic in an orderly fashion. You first can develop main topics or ideas. Underneath each of the main topics, you can describe the details associated with that topic using subtopics.

One of your daily teaching tools is your lesson plan. In this plan, you outline the main topics to be covered in the day's lesson and then put down the key points that need to be covered to teach that lesson.

Microsoft Word's outline features can assist you in developing lesson plans and handouts all at the same time. Your handouts are developed in the Page Layout View while your lesson plans are developed in the Outline View.

To view your document as an outline, click the **Outline View** button at the bottom left of your screen.

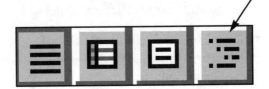

To look at your document in the **Page Layout View**, click the button to the left.

Notice that the toolbar changes and adds the Outline toolbar.

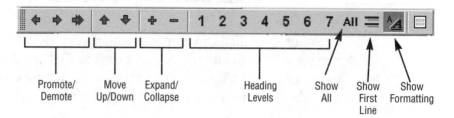

The **Promote/Demote** buttons let you change a topic from a main topic to a subtopic and vice versa.

Move Up/Down buttons help your reorganize your topics. You may decide that you need to rearrange how your details are listed. You can move the topic up through the list without using **Cut** and **Paste**.

The **Expand/Collapse** buttons let you determine what amount of detail you want to see on the page. For example, if you are doing a coversheet for a lesson plan, you may decide you only need the first and second level headings to show. Inside your document, you would show all levels of detail for teaching the topic.

Show Heading, **Show All Headings**, and **Show First Line Only** lets you automatically designate what level of heading or headings you want to show.

Show Formatting turns on and off the formatting in the Outline View. You may wish to have a clean outline that does not show different fonts and font styles.

Today's topic is "Removing Lint from the Lint Trap." You will create an outline for teaching this very important topic.

Try This:

- Start a new document using *New* from the **FILE** menu.
- Click the **Outline View**.
- Type in the following list.

Main topic: *(Removing Lint from the Lint Trap*

Subtopic: *What is lint?*

Where does lint come from?

Why is it important to remove?

Dryer lint traps

Techniques for removal

Clean-up techniques)

- All of these entries are at the same level in the document.

> □ *Removing Lint from the Lint Trap*
> □ What is lint?
> □ Where does lint come from?
> □ Why is it important to remove?
> □ Dryer lint traps
> □ Techniques for removal
> □ Clean-up techniques

The **Page Layout View** of the document looks like this:

> *Removing Lint from the Lint Trap*
> What is lint?
> Where does lint come from?
> Why is it important to remove?
> Dryer lint traps
> Techniques for removal
> Clean-up techniques

To make the top line of the document into a major heading (Heading 1), you will need to promote the line.

- To promote the first line to the major topic, select the line and click the **Promote** button.

  ○ *Removing Lint from the Lint Trap*
  - What is lint?
  - Where does lint come from?
  - Why is it important to remove?
  - Dryer lint traps
  - Techniques for removal
  - Clean-up techniques

- With the **Show Formatting** button activated, the first line becomes larger, moves to the left, and is designated with a ⊹ sign.

- Select the subtopic and click the right arrow, or **Demote** button, to demote the subtopic under the major topic, making it a Heading 2.

- Now select the second subtopic *(Dryer lint traps).* Because it is a subtopic under *(What is lint?),* you must click the **Promote** button to make it a Heading 2 also.

This example has three heading levels.

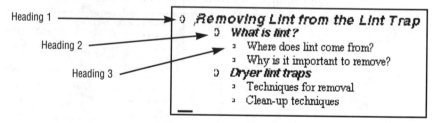

You can view your outline using the **Heading Level** buttons on your toolbar. This view has **Heading Level 2** selected. Notice that the sub-subtopics, or Heading 3, are not visible in this view.

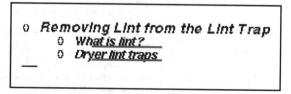

To print your outline, make sure you are viewing the outline, as you want it printed. If you only want to see Heading 1 and Heading 2, select them prior to sending the document to the printer. If you want to see your entire outline, click the **All** button prior to printing.

Tips for Success:

Look at the **Page Layout View** of the document. You can see that the main topic, subtopics, and sub-subtopics have different formatting. Remember that you can turn off this formatting on your Outline toolbar.

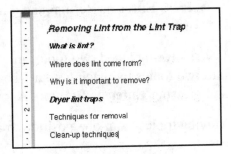

Add additional information to this page in the Page Layout View. *Microsoft Word* will treat the new information as sub-sub-subtopics and put them at Heading Level 4.

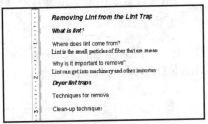

Page Layout View

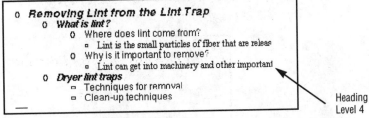

Outline View

Editing Outlines

In the previous lesson, using both the Outline View and the Page Layout View, you learned to adjust your outlines easily. Now look at two additional ways you can edit your outline.

Try This:

- To add or insert a topic into your outline, place your insertion point at the end of the line before the location where you want to add the topic.
- Press **Enter** or **Return** and a line is inserted. Type in your new topic.

If you have included two topics in one line, you can break them into two topics by placing your I-beam at the end of the first topic and pressing **Enter** or **Return**. Another new line is inserted.

Moving topics from one position to another in your outline is very easy.

- To move a topic up in the list, click **Show All** to display all of the lines of the outline.
- Select the line you wish to move.
- Click the **Move Up** arrow on the toolbar.

The topic moves up one line for each time your click the arrow. **Move Down** moves the topic down one line per click.

Activity #21: Just the Main Points Please!

The Outline View is a clean, uncomplicated way of looking at your document. Outlines let you set out the roadmap without cluttering up the view and possibly changing the direction of the project.

This information is the outline for a chapter in a book.

1. Open a *New* document from the **FILE** menu.
2. Type in the following lines:

   (Maintaining your car
   Engine oil
   Brands and grade
   Oil filters
   Frequency of change
   Tires
   Air
   Tread
   Water levels
   Antifreeze
   Hoses)

3. Click the **Outline View** layout button.
4. Promote the first line to the major topic.
5. Place lines 2, 6, and 9 at Heading Level 2.
6. Place all remaining lines at Heading Level 3.
7. Display your outline in the following ways by clicking the appropriate buttons.

   - **Show All**
   - **Show Heading Level 1**
   - **Show Heading Level 2**

You can see how handy *Microsoft Word*'s outlines can be for your lesson plans.

See an example on the CD-ROM (173act21.doc).

Creating a Second Document

You can start a new document while working on another document with *Microsoft Word* and have both opened at the same time.

Try This:

- To start a new document, click **FILE** from the menu bar.
- Click *New*.

You now have a new document open and active. The first document is in the background, open but inactive.

Switching Between Documents

While you have two or more documents open, you can switch back and forth between them.

- To change to another document that is open, click **WINDOW** on your menu bar.
- Click the name of the document that you want to be active. If you have not named the documents, they will be *Document1* and *Document2*.

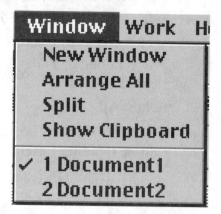

Note that the document that is currently on the screen has a checkmark to the left of the name. The name also shows at the top of the screen (Windows) or on the title bar (Macintosh).

Moving Text between Documents

You can move blocks of text from one document to another by using Cut and Paste.

Try This:

- Select **FILE** and then *Open*, to open the two documents you will be using.
- Select the text you wish to move.
- Click **EDIT** from the menu bar.
- Select *Cut*.
- Click **WINDOW** from the menu bar.
- Select the second document where you want the text to be moved.
- Insert the I-beam at the point where you want the text to be inserted.
- Click **EDIT**.
- Click *Paste*.

Tips for Success:

Undo works here also. If you do not like the move, just choose *Undo* from the **EDIT** menu.

Activity #22: A Little of This and a Little of That

It is time for a little fun. Use the files on your activity CD-ROM to do the following activity.

1. Open a new document by clicking **FILE**, and selecting *New*.

2. Use **WINDOW** from the menu bar, and select *Split* to divide the screen in two.

3. Click the left mouse button at the place where you want the screen split (Windows only).

4. Click in the top screen.

5. Click **INSERT** on the menu bar and select *FILE*. Open (Moving.doc) from the CD-ROM.

6. Scroll down in the top screen until you see the instructions for moving to the beginning of a paragraph.

7. Click the bottom screen and scroll until you see the instructions for moving to the top of the current screen.

The split screen is very handy when you are working with a very long document and need to see different places in the document at the same time.

Working with Documents Saved in Different Formats

Microsoft Word can open documents that have been created in several other formats.

Try This:

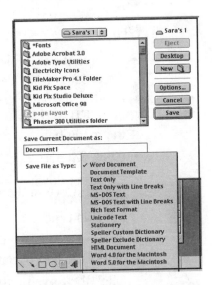

- To see the different formats that *Microsoft Word* can read, click **FILE**.
- Click *Open*.
- Click the arrow in the **List Files of Type** box.
- Scroll through the box to see if the type of file you need is listed. If so, click that file type.
- Select the file in the file list at the top of the dialog box.
- Click **Open**.

Microsoft Word will attempt to open the file. If it is unable to open the file as a *Microsoft Word* document, you will get a screen with "machine language" that may look like this.

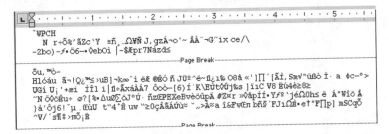

Saving Documents in Different Formats

You can save the documents you have created in *Microsoft Word* to be used in other programs and file formats.

Try This:

- To save the document in another format, click **FILE** from the menu bar.

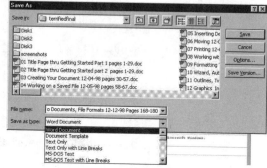

- Click *Save As*.
- Click the down arrow on the **Save as type** box.
- Select the appropriate file format.
- Click the **Save** button.

Tips for Success:

Some of the file formats in which you can save your *Microsoft Word* documents are:

Text

Microsoft Word (many versions)

Microsoft Works

Rich Text Format

WordPerfect (many versions)

HTML for Web Pages

Activity #23 Working Together
(Windows Only)

If you work on team projects involving many people, you may have the opportunity and need to use files from other word processing programs. *Microsoft Word* is very flexible and can read files from most major word processing programs.

For this activity, you are going to open a file that was created in *Corel WordPerfect 6.1*.

1. Click the **FILE** menu, then choose *Open*.

2. Select **All Files** in the **List Files of Type** box.

3. Select *(Activi23.wpd)*.

4. Click the **Open** button.

Microsoft Word will convert the file and open it with ease. Now you can save the file.

5. Choose *Save* from the **FILE** menu.

6. *Microsoft Word* will ask you if you want to save the document as a *Microsoft Word* document.

7. Click **Yes**.

The document is now a *Microsoft Word* document. To save it back to a *Corel WordPerfect* document, you will need to use **FILE**, then *Save As* and choose the *Corel WordPerfect* format.

Inserting Images

A picture really is worth a thousand words! If you were teaching a unit on space exploration, this picture could bring the topic to life. It shows the immense structure required to launch the shuttle.

This photo is out of a purchased package of art and photos that can be inserted into any document and does not require permission from the publisher. Using visuals in your projects and lessons can enhance learning and can also be fun. To insert a photo, you use the same copy and paste technique that you learned earlier.

Try This:

- Find the picture you want to insert into your document from graphic files on your computer.

- Press **Ctrl** + **C** (Windows) or ⌘ + **C** (Macintosh) to copy the photo.

- Return to the document you are creating.

- Place the insertion point where you want the picture inserted.
- Press **Ctrl + V** (Windows) or ⌘ + **V** (Macintosh) to paste the photo into your document.

Later you will learn how to resize and move the photo around in your document.

Tips for Success:

You can use several different methods to load images into your documents. Scanners allow you to scan a picture directly into your computer. These pictures can be photos, pictures from books, advertisements, or almost any other printed item.

Digital cameras take pictures that can be downloaded, saved on your computer, then put into your documents. Pictures can be found on the Internet as well. As with all literature and media, verify that the pictures you use are either free for public use or acquire permission to use them.

The most common file formats in which images can be saved on your computer are *.bmp (*Windows* bitmap), *.gif, and *.tif. Graphic files (image files) are often very large and can be slow to access; this will cause your computer to bog down. Be aware that the larger the graphic file, the more difficulty your computer and software may have in getting it all to work together.

Just remember that the time you spend adding graphics to your projects is time well spent. You will have fun, and your students will benefit.

Inserting Simple Shapes

In *Microsoft Word*, you are only two clicks away from adding several simple shapes to your documents. The **AutoShapes** button is available on your toolbar (Windows) or on the Drawing toolbar (Macintosh). To access the Drawing toolbar,  click the **Draw** button on the toolbar or select **INSERT** from the menu bar. Choose *Picture* from the drop down menu, and then choose **AutoShapes**. AutoShapes contains several types of commonly used shapes that can add excitement to your documents.

 Try This:

- To insert a shape into your document, click **AutoShapes**.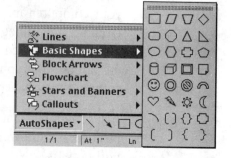
- Select the category of shapes that you want to use.
- Select the shape from the selection box by placing your mouse over the shape and clicking the mouse (Macintosh) or the left mouse button (Windows).
- The mouse arrow will become a +. Place the + at the location where you want to insert the shape.
- Hold down the left mouse button and drag the mouse until the shape is the size you want it to be.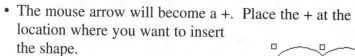
- Release the mouse button.

Tips for Success:

When you click the shape in your document, the handles appear. These are eight little squares positioned all around your shape. The little squares outline the area that the shape covers and can be used to resize the shape.

You can move the shape in your document by clicking it until the handles appear, then holding down the left mouse button (the arrow becomes a crossbar), drag the shape to its new location.

One of the options on the Drawing toolbar allows you to give your basic shape a 3-D effect.

To add the 3-D effect to your shape:

- Select the shape you want to use.
- Click the **3-D** tool button.
- Choose the 3-D effect you want from the selection box.

Watch your shape change. If you do not like this effect, you can use **Undo** from the **EDIT** menu if you have not saved or closed the document.

If you need to delete the 3-D effect:

- Click the shape to select it.

- Click the **3-D** tool button.

- Click **No 3-D** and the shape will return to its basic form.

You can also use Shadow effects on your shapes. Just as with the 3-D effects:

- Click your shape to select it.

- Click the **Shadow** tool button on your toolbar.

- A selection box will appear. Select the shadow effect you wish to use.

The effect is applied to your shape. To cancel or delete the effect, select **No Shadow** from the **Shadow** effects box.

Word Wrapping

As you read through this book, you might have noticed that paragraphs are wrapped around the shapes and screen examples. This is called text or word wrapping. You can select the type of wrap to be used in a certain situation by first selecting the shape and then selecting the **Text Wrapping** tool from the **Picture** toolbar.

You can also choose text wrapping for your simple shapes from the *AutoShapes* menu under **FORMAT**. In the **AutoShapes** dialog box you will have two options. You can select which wrapping style to use, and where you would like the text to be placed.

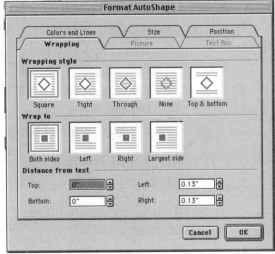

Tips for Success:

Use the **Text Wrapping** tool to give your projects a more professional layout and appearance.

Text Wrapping can be very helpful in columnar newsletters where maximizing space usage is very important.

Fun Symbols

How many times have you been typing along and wished you could use a symbol in your document? *Microsoft Word* lets you insert many common symbols and several *fun* symbols easily.

Try This:

- To insert a symbol into your document, click the **INSERT** menu.

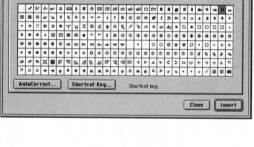

- Click *Symbol*.

- Select a symbol from the dialog box.

- Click the **Insert** button.

- Click the **Cancel** button to close the **Symbol** dialog box.

Your selection is now inserted into your document.

To make the symbol larger, increase the font size.

Note: You can change the sets of symbols by changing the Font style.

Under the **Special Characters** tab in the **Symbol** dialog box, you will find additional commonly used symbols that you can insert into your document.

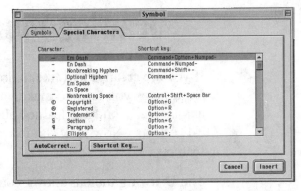

Tips for Success:

Microsoft Word has more fun symbols available in **AutoCorrect**. You can see a list of these symbols under *AutoCorrect* from the **TOOLS** menu.

As you type in each of these groups of characters, *Microsoft Word* automatically turns them into the fun symbols.

Drawing Your Own Picture

If you are creative and like to draw your own pictures, *Microsoft Word* gives you tools to make your drawing more fun and automated. You have learned about AutoShapes, Shadows, and 3-D effects. Now look at a few more of *Microsoft Word*'s features.

The **Drawing** toolbar allows you to do several basic drawing functions through its features. To activate the **Drawing** toolbar, select **VIEW** from the menu bar. Go to *Toolbars* and select the *Drawing* toolbar.

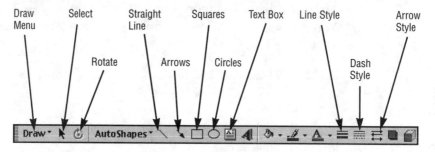

The **Draw** menu gives you the following options:

Grouping allows you to combine several objects together to edit or move them as one.

Order moves objects forward or backward so that they are in front or behind another object.

Grid helps *Microsoft Word* keep all of the objects lined up and even.

Nudge, **Align or Distribute**, and **Rotate or Flip** let you manipulate the object into the correct position.

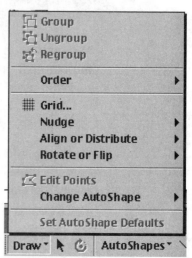

The **Select** button assists you in grabbing the object.

The **Rotate** button is useful in changing the horizontal and vertical position of an object.

Try This:

- Once you have selected an object, note that the handles, tiny boxes, appear. Click the **Rotate** button on the toolbar. The boxes are replaced by green dots.

- Place your mouse over one of these green dots and hold down the left mouse button while you rotate the object into a new position.

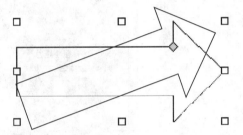

The **Line**, **Arrow**, **Rectangle**, and **Oval** tools allow you to draw each item with ease.

Try This:

- Simply choose one of the tool buttons and the mouse arrow becomes a (+).

- Click and hold down the left mouse button at the location where you want to insert the object.

- Drag the (+) until you get the shape you want.

- Release the mouse button.

A **Text Box** lets you insert words, such as labels, in any area of your document.

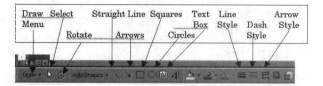

The text box is inserted using the same technique you used for squares and circles and can be formatted by selecting *Text Box* from the **FORMAT** menu.

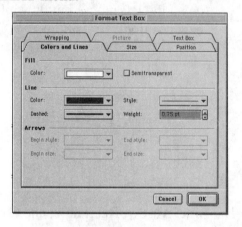

To use the **Line Style**, **Dash Style**, and **Arrow Style** buttons, first use the Line or Arrow tool to draw your line. Then, select the line to edit it. Click the **Line**, **Dash**, or **Arrow Style** button and choose the style you want from their list. Your line will change as soon as you click the left mouse button (Windows) or release the mouse (Macintosh).

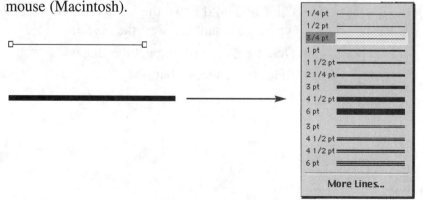

Activity #24: Picture This!

Here is a fun little project for you. Using the tools that you have just mastered, draw a gingerbread house. A starter house can be found on your CD-ROM (191act24.doc).

Here are some suggestions:

1. Use **AutoShapes** for the structure.

2. Draw fences and trees.

3. Add symbols for decorations.

4. Use different colors and font sizes.

5. Be creative and play a little. You deserve it!

Clip Art

Clip art is a collection of pictures that you can use in your documents. Several pieces of clip art come with *Microsoft Word*.

Try This:

- To look at and insert a picture from the clip art collection in *Microsoft Word*, click **INSERT**.

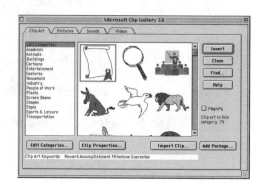

- Select *Picture* and then *Clip Art* from the drop down menus.

- The **Microsoft Clip Gallery** dialog box appears.

- Scroll through the pictures until you find one that meets your needs. Notice that the pictures are divided into categories to help you find a picture faster.

- Click the **Insert** button. The **Microsoft Clip Gallery** dialog box closes, and the picture is inserted into your document.

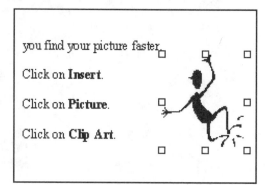

- Use the handles to size and move your clip art.

To delete clip art from your document:

- Select the clip art by clicking it with your left mouse button (Windows) or mouse button (Macintosh).

- Press the **Delete** key.

Tips for Success:

Many software publishers include clip art in their programs. Some come with a printed catalog and others use a cataloging system on the computer. A handy tool for your classroom is a clip art collection. This collection has as many as 600,000 different pictures and is stored on a series of CD-ROM discs.

Clip art files are available in both color and black and white. The color pictures are great to use in computer presentations and to print if you have a color printer. If your printer is black and white, you will need to print a test sheet to see of the artwork is clear enough to use in your document.

You can also get clip art files from the Web. Be careful not to use pictures that are marked © Copyrighted. These pictures require the permission of the artist before they can be used.

Clip art can add direction to your document and contribute to the communication of ideas in your lesson plans.

Importing Pictures

When you think of clip art, you probably think primarily of drawings and artists' renditions of items. However, included in many clip art collections are photos that are also available for your use. You will enjoy using these photos until the cows come home.

You can also import pictures into your documents from other files or from a scanner.

Scan a photo and save it as a *.gif, *.tif, or *.bmp file. Then, insert the picture into your document.

Try This:

- Click **INSERT** from the menu bar.

- Select *Picture* from the drop down menu.

- Click *From File*.

- Scroll through the files listed to see the previews of each file.

- Once you have found the file you want to use, click the **Insert** button, and the picture will be inserted into your document.

Tips for Success:

After you have imported pictures into *Microsoft Word*, you can adjust the image, contrast, and brightness. The Picture toolbar will automatically appear when an image is inserted into your document. You can also find the Picture toolbar under the **VIEW** menu, then choose *Toolbars* and select the *Picture* toolbar.

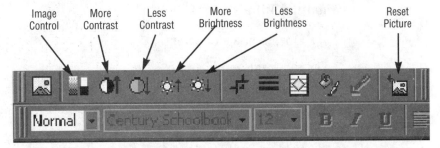

Take another look at the cows, and use each of the **Image Control** settings.

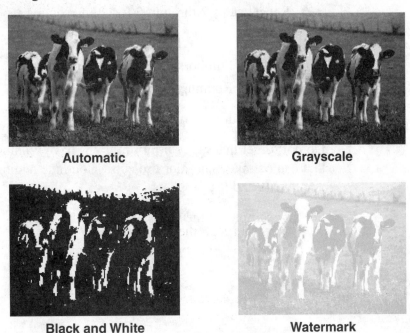

If you change your mind and want to return to the original picture, click the **Reset Picture** button.

Activity #25: Adding Some Spice

Clip art, color and pictures bring your documents to life; they add spice to the written word. Use graphics to add meaning and increase understanding.

For this activity, practice using clip art by selecting images from *Microsoft Word*'s **Clip Gallery**.

1. Open a new document.

2. Click **INSERT**, and then *Pictures* from the drop down menu.

3. Select **Clip Art**.

4. Select pictures that communicate the word "splat."

5. Click the **Insert** button.

6. Repeat steps 2 through 5 for the following words.

> No Way!
>
> Stubborn
>
> Running in Circles

7. Label your selections *(Activity#25)*.

Do not forget that many print programs have volumes of clip art that can complement your projects. Continue adding spice to your documents and lesson plans.

See an example on the CD-ROM (196act25.doc).

Resizing, Moving, and Cropping Images

Microsoft Word is very flexible and lets you move and resize images easily. If you do not like the adjustments you made to an image, use *Undo* from the **EDIT** menu to undo the most recent adjustment. If you want to restart with the original image, click the **Reset Picture** button.

Try This:

- To resize an image, click the image to select it.

- Click and hold down the mouse button while pointing at one of the handles.

- Drag the handle until the image reaches the size you desire.

- Release the mouse button.

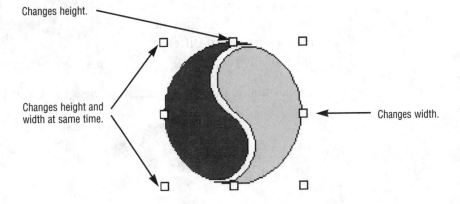

Changes height.

Changes height and width at same time.

Changes width.

Try This:

- To move an image, click the image and hold down the mouse button (Macintosh) or left mouse button (Windows). The arrow will turn into a crossbar.

- Drag the image to the new location.

- Release the mouse button.

If your picture has extra edges or unwanted parts, you can cut those parts off of the picture by using the cropping tool.

Try This:

- To crop (or trim) a picture, click the picture so that the handles will show.

- Click the **Crop** tool.

- Click a handle and hold down the mouse button.

- Drag the handle until you see the dotted line at the place where you want to trim the picture. Use different handles to cut off different sides of the picture.

- Click outside the image area to release the **Crop** tool.

Moving Tables

Tables can be moved from one area of your document to another using **Cut** and **Paste**.

School	Students	Teachers
Moore	985	66
Corey	874	62
Wood	960	63

Try This:

If you want to move this table lower in the document, or to another document:

- Select the table by clicking in the left margin and holding down the left mouse button.

- Drag the mouse down until the entire table is selected.

- Click **EDIT.**

- Click *Cut*.

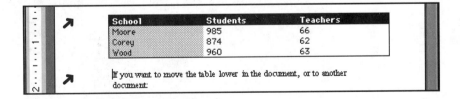

- Position your I-beam where you want to insert the table.

- Select *Paste* from the **EDIT** menu.

Your table is now in its new location.

Activity #26: Take a Look at These Figures

Putting a table in your presentation is easy and a great way to communicate facts and figures. If you write proposals, you will find inserting tables an absolute necessity.

1. Open a new document and type the following:

(Increase Reading Interest in Your Classroom. Feedback is the key to getting your second graders to increase their interest in reading. Use a Reading Log to keep track of your students' reading and to encourage participation.)

2. Open (200act26.doc) from the CD-ROM.

3. Select the table.

4. Click **EDIT** and then *Copy*.

5. Click **WINDOW** from the menu bar and switch to your first document.

6. Place your I-beam at the point where you want to insert the table.

7. Click **EDIT** and then *Paste*.

Good job. You have just copied a table from one document to another.

WordArt

WordArt is a function that allows you to use color and design to make your titles fancy.

Try This:

- To use WordArt, click the **WordArt** button on your **Drawing** toolbar.

- If the **Drawing** toolbar is not visible, select **VIEW** from the menu bar. Choose *Toolbars* and then *Drawing* from the drop down menus.

- When the **WordArt Gallery** dialog box appears, select a style for your WordArt.

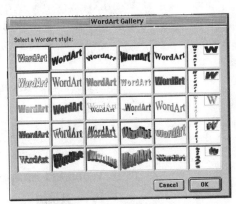

- Click the **OK** button.

- When the **Edit WordArt Text** box appears, fill in your text.

- Click **OK**.

Your text will appear in the WordArt form that you selected. WordArt will give you handles to adjust the image. A toolbar will also appear for making changes to the image.

The options included on the toolbar are:

- **Insert WordArt**
- **Edit Text**
- **WordArt Gallery**
- **Format WordArt**
- **WordArt Shape**
- **Free Rotate**
- **WordArt Same Letter Heights**
- **WordArt Vertical Text**
- **WordArt Alignment**
- **WordArt Character Spacing**

Tips for Success:

WordArt can be a great addition to cover sheets and certificates. If you have a color printer, the design and color used in WordArt will add excitement to your projects.

Borders and Shading

The Borders feature of *Microsoft Word* lets you set off portions of your document to bring attention to the text. You saw many of the Border features while learning about tables. Now you will see how borders can be used with regular text.

Try This:

- Type the following:

Bring the following supplies to school on Monday:
1. Pencil
2. Paper
3. Ruler
4. Calculator
5. Math book

- Select the text you want to surround with the border.
- Click **FORMAT**.
- Click *Borders and Shading* and a dialog box appears.
- The **Borders** tab is used for paragraphs.
- The **Page Border** tab is used to put a border around an entire page.

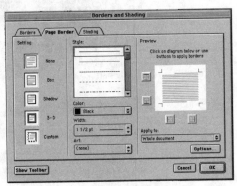

- Select a type of **Border Setting** and **Style**, then preview it in the **Preview** box.
- Click **OK**.

Tips for Success:

Use shading to accentuate important details in your document. In the previous example, if the list of supplies is buried in a multi-page letter describing standardized testing that the students will be taking, you may want to make sure that the parents see this list.

Try This:

To make the list stand out further, use shading.

- Select the text you want to surround with the border.
- Click **FORMAT**.
- Click *Borders and Shading*.
- Click the **Shading** tab.
- Select the amount of gray fill or color you want to use as shading.
- Click **OK**.

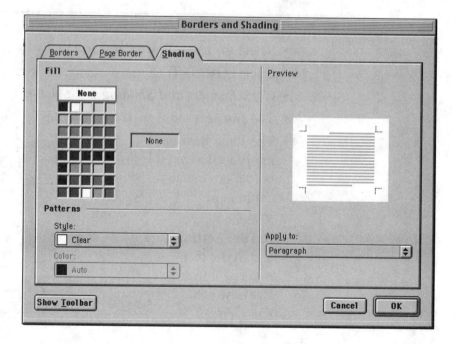

Bring the following supplies to school on Monday:
1. Pencil
2. Paper
3. Ruler
4. Calculator
5. Math book

Now the information stands out from the document and will be more noticeable to the reader. You can change **Fill Color**, **Line Color**, and **Font Color** using the **Drawing** toolbar.

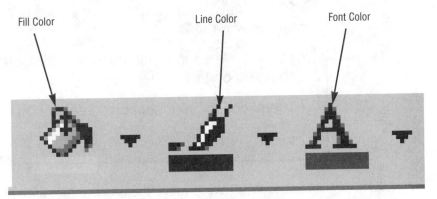

Fill Color   Line Color   Font Color

Most of the formatting features in *Microsoft Word* allow you to change the color. If you are doing an on-screen presentation or have access to a color printer, color can significantly enhance your project, grab attention, and emphasize important points.

Activity #27: Complete This Picture

Go back to your note to the parents announcing Field Days. How can you dress it up even more?

Field Days

May 6, 7, and 8

Our class will be competing in Field Days on Tuesday, May 6. The class voted to wear blue t-shirts and blue jean shorts as our class uniform. Please have your student wear shoes appropriate for running races.

You are invited to watch our class compete and cheer us on to victory.

Thank you for your support. See you on the 6th.

---

1. Add WordArt to make the title brighter and more colorful.
2. Make the words *(blue t-shirts)* blue in color.
3. Find a piece of clip art that communicates information about the event.
4. Add any other special touches that you think will complete the picture.

Remember—
Grab attention using color, graphics,
and cool effects.

See an example on the CD-ROM (206act27.doc).

Classroom Activities

This section of the book includes projects for your students to complete using some of the features available in *Microsoft Word*. A checklist following each activity identifies the skills they will practice.

Taboo Short Stories

Objective:

Students use creative writing skills and develop vocabulary.

Resources:

List of taboo words

Procedure:

1. Write a list of related words related to Thanksgiving on the board: turkey, pumpkin pie, Pilgrims, feast, share, etc. Tell students that for today, these words are "taboo" and they may not use them in their writing.

2. Discuss synonyms and different ways of expressing the same idea. Telll students that they will be using synonyms for the words traditionally found in stories about Thanksgiving.

3. Have students open *Microsoft Word* and create a new blank document.

4. Have students write a short story about Thanksgiving without using any of the taboo words on the list.

5. If students have trouble thinking of synonyms, have them use the Thesaurus in *Microsoft Word*.

   a. Highlight the word for which you need a synonym.

   b. Click **TOOLS** on the menu bar.

Taboo Short Stories *(cont.)*

    c. Put your pointer on ***Language***.

    d. Select ***Thesaurus*** from the drop down menu.

    e. If there are synonyms in the *Microsoft Word* dictionary, they will be displayed. Replace the highlighted word by selecting the synonym and then clicking the **Replace** button.

    f. If a student does not know the meaning of one of the words on the list, they can highlight it and click the **Look Up** button. Another list of synonyms, including parts of speech, will appear.

6. Have students proofread their stories.

7. Have students run Spell Check on their stories.

8. Have students save their stories to a floppy disk.

    a. Click **FILE**, then *Save As*.

    b. (Windows) Click the **Save in** box, and select **3½ floppy A** or whatever letter represents your floppy disk drive.

    c. (Macintosh) Select the **floppy disk** icon from your desktop and click the **Open** button.

    d. Name their file in the **Save Current Document As:** box.

    e. Click the **Save** button.

Word Processing Skills

Skill Area	Specific Skill	✔
Access a file	Open a file	
	Create a file	✔
	Save a file	✔
Enter text	Insert text using word wrap and return appropriately	✔
	Use shift key for capital letters	✔
Moving through a document	Use arrow keys/mouse to move cursor in document	✔
	Scroll through document	
Edit text	Delete text	
	Cut/copy/paste text	
	Search/replace text	
	Move text	
	Insert text	
	Select text	
	Spell check	✔
Manipulate format	Select/change font or font size	
	Select/change justification	
	Select/change spacing	
	Select/change indention	
	Use page numbers	
	Create outlines	
	Use tables	
	Use columns	
	Format envelopes/labels	
	Set/move tabs	
	Create/set margins	
Using Graphics	Insert images	
	Insert simple shapes	
	Import images	
	Clip Art	
	Move and resize	
	WordArt/Borders/Shading	
Print	Select print command	
	Select print options	

Letters to the President or First Lady

Objective:

Students learn to write formal letters.

Students develop, increase, and practice word processing skills.

Resources:

Rules for writing formal letters

Notes on questions to ask

on the CD-ROM (210plett.doc)

Procedure:

1. Discuss with the class the rules for writing a formal letter.

2. Discuss with the class ideas for questions to ask the President or First Lady. The students should jot down ideas that appeal to them.

   a. How did you decide what to have in the sculpture garden?

   b. What are your pets' names?

   c. What made you decide to be President?

   d. Is being the First Lady harder than being a lawyer?

   e. Can you redecorate your bedroom?

   f. How do you decide who will be in the Cabinet?

   g. What were the reasons you chose the vice-presidential candidate you did?

   h. What is your favorite job? least favorite job?

Letters to the President or First Lady *(cont.)*

3. Have students create a new document, and set the top margin at 2.5 inches.

   a. Click **FILE** on the menu bar.

   b. Click *Page Setup* on the drop down menu.

   c. Click the **Margins** tab and set the top margin.

4. Have students set the tabs for the return address, closing, and name if using the modified block style.

   a. Click the little button at the far left of the horizontal ruler until it changes to the type of tab you want to insert. In this case it needs to be a left tab.

   b. Click the horizontal ruler where you want to set a tab stop.

Note: If you want to set precise measurements for tabs, choose *Tabs* from the **FORMAT** menu.

5. Have students enter the text.

6. Have students proofread and spell check.

7. Have students edit and correct if necessary.

8. Have students save their files to floppy disks.

9. Have students print their letters.

Box 776
Anywhere, USA
April 8, 200-

President Bill Clinton
Pennsylvania Ave.
Washington, DC

Dear Mr. President:

Xxxxxx xxxxxx xxx xxx xx xxxxxxx xxxxx xxx xxx
Xxxx xxxx xxx xxx xxx xxx xx.

Yyyyy yyyy yyy yyyy yyyyy yyy yy yyy yyyyy yy
Yyyy yyyyyy yyy yyyyy yyyy yyyyy yyyy yyy .

Sincerely,

Jame Doe

Word Processing Skills

Skill Area	Specific Skill	✔
Access a file	Open a file	
	Create a file	✔
	Save a file	✔
Enter text	Insert text using word wrap and return appropriately	✔
	Use shift key for capital letters	✔
Moving through a document	Use arrow keys/mouse to move cursor in document	✔
	Scroll through document	✔
Edit text	Delete text	
	Cut/copy/paste text	
	Search/replace text	
	Move text	
	Insert text	
	Select text	
	Spell check	✔
Manipulate format	Select/change font or font size	
	Select/change justification	
	Select/change spacing	
	Select/change indention	
	Use page numbers	
	Create outlines	
	Use tables	
	Use columns	
	Format envelopes/labels	
	Set/move tabs	✔
	Create/set margins	✔
Using Graphics	Insert images	
	Insert simple shapes	
	Import images	
	Clip Art	
	Move and resize	
	WordArt/Borders/Shading	
Print	Select print command	✔
	Select print options	✔

Envelopes

Objective:

Students learn how to create envelopes to accompany the letters they have just written.

Resources:

File containing the letter to the President or First Lady

Example on the CD-ROM (210plett.doc)

Procedure:

1. Have the students open the letter they wrote in the Letters to the President or First Lady activity.

   a. Select *Open* from the **FILE** menu or click the **Open** icon on the Standard Toolbar.

   b. (Windows) In the dialog box that appears, click in the box beside **Look in** and choose **3¹/₂ floppy A** (or whatever letter your disk drive is). (Macintosh) Select the **floppy disk** icon from your desktop and click the **Open** button.

   c. Select the name of the file you want to open.

   d. Click the **Open** button.

2. When the letter appears on the screen, students should click **TOOLS** on the menu bar.

3. Select *Envelopes and Labels*.

4. Click the **Envelopes** tab.

5. The mailing address should be in the address box.

6. Students should change the return address to their own or the school's address.

Note: Point out that if this were their own computer, and they were the only ones using it, the return address would not have to be re-entered each time.

Envelopes *(cont.)*

8. Click the **Options** button.

9. Select the **Envelope Options** tab.

10. Make sure the envelope size is correct.

11. Click the **Printing Options** tab.

12. Make sure the way your printer feeds envelopes is highlighted.

13. Click the **OK** button.

14. Put an envelope into the printer.

15. Click the **Print** button.

Word Processing Skills

Skill Area	Specific Skill	✓
Access a file	Open a file	✓
	Create a file	
	Save a file	
Enter text	Insert text using word wrap and return appropriately	✓
	Use shift key for capital letters	✓
Moving through a document	Use arrow keys/mouse to move cursor in document	✓
	Scroll through document	
Edit text	Delete text	✓
	Cut/copy/paste text	
	Search/replace text	
	Move text	
	Insert text	
	Select text	
	Spell check	
Manipulate format	Select/change font or font size	
	Select/change justification	
	Select/change spacing	
	Select/change indention	
	Use page numbers	
	Create outlines	
	Use tables	
	Use columns	
	Format envelopes/labels	✓
	Set/move tabs	
	Create/set margins	
Using Graphics	Insert images	
	Insert simple shapes	
	Import images	
	Clip Art	
	Move and resize	
	WordArt/Borders/Shading	
Print	Select print command	✓
	Select print options	✓

Book of Family Stories— Part One

Objective:

Students gain interviewing skills.

Students improve word processing skills.

Students learn new formatting techniques.

Resources:

Family members and old friends

Procedure:

1. Have students interview family members or old friends for family history stories.

2. Have students use a tape recorder if one is available.

    a. Keep in mind, however, that tape recorders make some people nervous. In that case, written notes would be preferable.

    b. If students do not use tape recorders, discuss note-taking techniques and tips for getting information down fast and accurately.

3. Students should have a list of questions or prompts to nudge their families' or friends' memories. A sample list is provided at the end of this activity.

4. Students should transcribe the notes or tapes as quickly as possible after the interview, in order not to lose any impressions gained by facial expressions and body language.

    a. Have the students create a blank document in *Microsoft Word*.

    b. They should type the information just as it is on the tape or in the notes. They will format it later.

Book of Family Stories— Part One *(cont.)*

5. Have students save the file on a floppy disk. Make sure that they give the file a different name than the one they will give to their final document.

6. The students should collect as many stories as possible. Sometimes several will be collected at one interview. Remind students that several short interviews are often better than one long one where everyone gets tired.

7. Be sure each file is given a different name. Sometimes students do not remember that a new file will replace an old file with the same name.

8. After the stories are collected, students should begin to put them together. This can be an on-going project throughout the school year if you choose.

9. Discuss with students the elements that make a story flow.

10. Have students open and print the files that contain the notes they have taken.

11. Have students create a new document.

12. Press **Ctrl + 2** (Windows) or ⌘ **+ 2** (Macintosh) to double-space.

Book of Family Stories—
Part One *(cont.)*

Encourage students to choose an easy-to-read font for the story titles.

    a. Click the down-pointing triangle beside the **Style** box on the Formatting toolbar. (It should say Normal now.)

    b. Choose **Title** (Windows) or **Heading 1** (Macintosh). *(This is a very important step.)*

    c. Click the **B** on the **Formatting** toolbar to make the title bold.

    d. Type the title to the first story and press **Enter** (Windows) or **Return** (Macintosh) twice.

14. Instruct students to enter the text of the first story.

15. Spell check and proofread. Edit if necessary.

16. Save the final copy on a disk.

17. Have students do the same for each story collected, making sure to give each story a different file name.

Word Processing Skills

Skill Area	Specific Skill	✓
Access a file	Open a file	✓
	Create a file	✓
	Save a file	✓
Enter text	Insert text using word wrap and return appropriately	✓
	Use shift key for capital letters	✓
Moving through a document	Use arrow keys/mouse to move cursor in document	✓
	Scroll through document	✓
Edit text	Delete text	
	Cut/copy/paste text	
	Search/replace text	
	Move text	
	Insert text	
	Select text	
	Spell check	✓
Manipulate format	Select/change font or font size	✓
	Select/change justification	
	Select/change spacing	✓
	Select/change indention	
	Use page numbers	
	Create outlines	
	Use tables	
	Use columns	
	Format envelopes/labels	
	Set/move tabs	
	Create/set margins	
Using Graphics	Insert images	
	Insert simple shapes	
	Import images	
	Clip Art	
	Move and resize	
	WordArt/Borders/Shading	
Print	Select print command	✓
	Select print options	✓

Book of Family Stories—
Part One *(cont.)*

Interview Tips:

Nearly any relative you choose will have a family story to tell. Once you have nudged their memories, one story leads to another, especially if you are with several members of your extended family.

Some stories do not need to go into your book if they will embarrass or hurt someone. Please be considerate.

Your book can also include poems or tales that have been a part of your family's history, even though they do not tell about your family directly.

The sample questions will help get you started on your interviews or make you think of topics of your own.

Be a good listener and always thank the person you are interviewing for their time and information.

Book of Family Stories—
Part One *(cont.)*

Sample Questions:

What is your full name and why were you named that?

Do/did you have a nickname? What is it and why were you called that?

Where was your first home?

What are your earliest memories?

What did your family do for fun?

What were your favorite games and toys when you were a child?

Were there any fads that were popular during your youth?

When you were a child, what did you want to be when you grew up?

Did you serve in the armed forces?

Where did you meet your wife/husband?

What did you do on dates?

What was the funniest thing any of your children ever did or said?

Has anyone ever saved your life?

Have you ever saved anyone's life?

What would you consider the most important invention during your lifetime?

Who was your best friend when you were young?

What do you remember best about him/her?

What were the hardest choices you ever had to make?

What was your favorite place you ever visited? Why?

What were holidays like in your family?

How did you celebrate birthdays?

Did you ever get in trouble at school?

What is the funniest thing that ever happened at school?

Did you have pets growing up? What was your favorite one?

When you were a child, who was your favorite relative? Why?

Book of Family Stories— Part Two

Objective:

Students improve word processing skills.

Students improve narrative writing skills.

Students learn how to include different types of images into documents.

Resources:

Family Story files

Comb binder (if available)

Scanner (if available)

Card Stock for cover

Procedure:

1. Have each student create a new blank document.
2. Press **Ctrl + 2** (Windows) or ⌘ **+ 2** (Macintosh) to double space.
3. Make this a title page. It should have the title of the book and the author's name.
4. Insert a page break after the last text on the title page.
   a. Click **INSERT** on the menu bar.
   b. Click *Break*.
   c. Click the little circle by **page break** and then click **OK**.
5. On the next page, click the **Center Alignment** button on the **Formatting** toolbar, the bar with the font and font size box on it. The alignment buttons have little horizontal lines on them.
   a. To make the title bold, click the **B** on the **Formatting** toolbar.
   b. Type *(Table of Contents)* in a nice, large, bold font.

Book of Family Stories—
Part Two *(cont.)*

6. Press **Enter** or **Return** several times and then insert another page break.

7. Click **INSERT** on the menu bar.

8. Click **File**.

9. Open the floppy disk and select the first story. Then click **OK**. The first story will be inserted into the document.

10. Insert a page break.

11. Repeat steps 6–10 for each story.

12. If students have photographs that they want to include, they can scan them, save the files to disk, and use them to illustrate their stories.

    a. Place the cursor at the point where the top of the photograph should be inserted.

    b. *Microsoft Word* can use most of the formats that students will encounter. If *Microsoft Word* cannot read files from the scanner, usually the scanner software will allow the pictures to be saved as a jpeg or a bitmap file that *Microsoft Word* can read.

    c. Click **INSERT** on the menu bar.

    d. Select *Picture* from the drop down menu.

    e. Click *From File*.

    f. Click the **Look in** box. (Windows)

    g. Locate your picture file, select it, and click **Insert**.

    h. The photograph will then appear in the document.

    i. Students can resize the picture by moving their pointer over the little squares on the corners of the image. When the pointer turns into a double headed arrow, they can hold the mouse button down and make the picture larger or smaller. The squares on the sides, top, and bottom work the same way, but students have to be careful not to lose the proportion.

Book of Family Stories— Part Two *(cont.)*

j. Students can move the image by moving the pointer over the interior of the image. When the pointer becomes a four-pointed arrow, they can hold down the mouse button and drag the image to another location. Their text will separate and move itself to wrap around the image.

k. Students can change the way the text wraps around the image by selecting **FORMAT**, then *Picture*, and clicking the **Wrapping** tab.

13. If students want to illustrate with drawings done in a program like *Microsoft Paint,* they can save the drawings to disk, and then follow the instructions above.

14. Some clip art is included with *Microsoft Word.* The students may find illustrations there that will fit their needs.

   a. Position the cursor.

   b. Click **INSERT** on the menu bar.

   c. Move your pointer to the word *Picture*.

   d. Select *Clip Art*.

   e. When students find the art they want to use, have them click it, and then click the **Insert** button.

   f. Resize and move according to instructions for moving photograph images.

15. Some students may want to illustrate their stories with images that they find on the Internet. They must make sure that using the images is not a copyright infringement. Most Web page authors do not mind as long as students are not using the images for commercial use, but it is safest to always ask permission. *(Disney does mind.)*

   a. To use an image from the Internet, place the pointer on the image and click and hold the mouse button (Macintosh) or right mouse button (Windows). Choose **Save Image As**, and save it to your disk.

Book of Family Stories—
Part Two *(cont.)*

b. Follow the instructions in Step 12 for inserting photographs.

c. Some good sites for art that students can have for personal non-commercial use are:

http://www.arttoday.com

This site is not free. There is a subscription fee of $29.95 per year, but it is well worth it.

http://webclipart.miningco.com

This site has several clip art collections and links to many, many more.

http://www.clipartconnection.com/

This site has an immense collection of clip art that is categorized to make it easier to find what you want.

16. Have students put a footer on each page that contains the page number. They do not have to actually put it on each page. Just do it once for the whole document.

a. Scroll down to the first page of the first story. Skip the title page and the table of contents page.

b. Click **VIEW** on the menu bar.

c. Click *Header and Footer*.

d. Scroll down and click inside the **Footer**.

e. Click the **Center Alignment** button on the **Formatting** toolbar. The alignment buttons have horizontal lines on them.

f. Click the **Insert Page Numbers** button on the **Header and Footer** toolbar. It should be in the center of the page right now.

Book of Family Stories— Part Two *(cont.)*

g. Click the **Page Setup** or **Document Layout** button on the **Header and Footer toolbar**. It looks like an open book.

h. In the dialog box, find the **Apply to:** box. Click the down triangle and choose **This point forward**. Click the **OK** button.

i. Close the **Header and Footer** toolbar. The page numbers will now appear at the bottom of each page in the center.

17. Have students make a table of contents for the book.

   a. Scroll up to the table of contents page.

   b. Place the cursor where the table of contents should begin.

   c. Click **INSERT** on the menu toolbar.

   d. Click **Index and Tables**, and then click the **Table of Contents** tab.

   e. Click the **Options** button.

   f. Under **Available Styles**, remove the numbers **1**, **2**, and **3** by **Heading 1**, **2**, and **3**. Scroll down until you see **Title** (Windows) or **Normal** (Macintosh), and put the number one in the box across from it.

   g. Click **OK**.

   h. Choose the type of **Tab** leader that will go from the titles to the page numbers.

   i. Click **OK**.

18. Have students save the final document after spell checking, proofreading, and editing.

19. Students should print the final documents.

20. Bind using a comb binder if one is available. If not, staple or put into 3-ring binders.

Word Processing Skills

Skill Area	Specific Skill	✓
Access a file	Open a file	✓
	Create a file	✓
	Save a file	✓
Enter text	Insert text using word wrap and return appropriately	✓
	Use shift key for capital letters	✓
Moving through a document	Use arrow keys/mouse to move cursor in document	✓
	Scroll through document	✓
Edit text	Delete text	
	Cut/copy/paste text	
	Search/replace text	
	Move text	
	Insert text	✓
	Select text	
	Spell check	✓
Manipulate format	Select/change font or font size	✓
	Select/change justification	✓
	Select/change spacing	✓
	Select/change indention	
	Use page numbers	✓
	Create outlines	
	Use tables	
	Use columns	
	Format envelopes/labels	
	Set/move tabs	
	Create/set margins	
Using Graphics	Insert images	✓
	Insert simple shapes	
	Import images	
	Clip Art	✓
	Move and resize	✓
	WordArt/Borders/Shading	
Print	Select print command	✓
	Select print options	✓

Publishing a Class Newspaper

Objective:

Students improve writing skills.

Students improve and increase word processing skills.

Resources:

Samples of newspapers

Example on the CD-ROM (228news1.doc)

Procedure:

1. Choose students to be editors. These should be students who are relatively good at spelling, grammar, and are not afraid of a dictionary.

2. Choose students to be reporters. Since the paper is extracurricular at most schools, get recommendations from other teachers about both editors and reporters. Keep in mind that reporters will have to miss class at times to do interviews, so they must be students who can make up missed class work easily.

3. You can have many reporters, and reporter teams work well. If you have some children who have trouble writing, pair them with students who can help with the writing. Often those who cannot seem to get their thoughts down on paper come up with the most creative stories when you remove the stress and fear of having to produce a written product.

Publishing a Class Newspaper *(cont.)*

4. Choose one or two students to be photographers. These students will also have to miss class occasionally. You should teach a lesson on the use of the digital camera or the scanner.

5. Choose students to be artists and illustrators.

6. Discuss with the class what sections the newspaper will contain. Students should look at various newspapers to see how they are organized.

7. Some typical sections for a school newspaper include the following:

   a. front page stories
   b. editorial page
   c. opinion page
   d. news stories
   e. gossip columns
   f. literary page
   g. book reviews
   h. original poetry & stories
   i. interviews
   j. sports

8. If you have a publishing program like *Microsoft Publisher* or *Broderbund Press Writer*, students can type their stories in *Microsoft Word* and then import them into the publishing program. That way you can avoid buying multiple copies of the publishing program.

9. If you do not have a publishing program, do not worry. I have been producing a very nice newspaper for several years with *Microsoft Word*. In fact, in some ways it is more versatile.

10. There are several ways to lay out a newspaper with *Microsoft Word*. Students will use tables for this activity.

Publishing a Class Newspaper *(cont.)*

11. Create a new blank document.

12. Students should set right and left margins to 1 inch.

    a. Click **FORMAT** on the menu bar.

    b. Choose *Document*, and then the Margins tab.

    c. Change the **Right** and **Left** margin settings.

    d. Click the **OK** button.

13. Using WordArt, students should make the banner.

    a. Click **INSERT** on the menu bar.

    b. Point to *Picture* on the drop down menu.

    c. Choose *WordArt*.

Or

    a. Click **VIEW** on the menu bar.

    b. Point to *Toolbars* on the drop down menu, and click **Drawing**.

    c. On the **Drawing** toolbar, click the three-dimensional **A** that represents **WordArt**.

14. Keep in mind that WordArt is a drawing object and is not treated as text.

15. Students should click where the text area should begin.

    a. Click **TABLE** on the menu bar

    b. Select *Draw Table*. The cursor will become a tiny pencil.

    c. Click and drag the pencil to form a rectangle the size of the paper's text area.

16. If the **Tables and Borders** toolbar is not visible, open it by clicking **VIEW**, and choosing *Toolbars*. Or students can click the **Tables and Borders** icon on the Standard toolbar. It is a little windowpane with a pencil in it.

17. Students should now draw the lines for columns and rows.

Publishing a Class
Newspaper *(cont.)*

18. Students should choose whether or not to have the column and row lines show.

    a. Click **TABLE** on the menu bar.

    b. Click *Select Table*.

    c. On the **Tables and Borders** toolbar click the **Borders** button. It is the little windowpane without a pencil.

    d. This will give students a drop down menu that will let them choose anything from **Full Borders** to **No Borders** for the whole table.

    e. To add borders to a specific cell, click inside a cell, and then click the **Borders** button.

19. To erase a line, click the **Eraser** button, and drag the eraser over the line. The **Eraser** is next to the **Pencil** on the **Tables and Borders** toolbar.

20. When students finish creating the table, they should select a cell and begin entering text or graphics.

21. Students should change the tabs to make a smaller paragraph indention.

22. Students should also use a different font or bold type on the first word of an article.

23. Students should use full justification to make the edges of their columns straight, but this might make the articles difficult to read.

    a. Click the **Justify** button on the **Formatting** toolbar before they begin typing.

Or

    b. Highlight the text to justify, and then click the **Justify** button on the **Formatting** toolbar.

24. Students should copy and paste the articles into the cells, or move them around after they are inserted into the cells.

25. Save often and print.

Word Processing Skills

Skill Area	Specific Skill	✓
Access a file	Open a file	✓
	Create a file	✓
	Save a file	✓
Enter text	Insert text using word wrap and return appropriately	✓
	Use shift key for capital letters	✓
Moving through a document	Use arrow keys/mouse to move cursor in document	✓
	Scroll through document	✓
Edit text	Delete text	
	Cut/copy/paste text	✓
	Search/replace text	
	Move text	✓
	Insert text	✓
	Select text	✓
	Spell check	✓
Manipulate format	Select/change font or font size	✓
	Select/change justification	✓
	Select/change spacing	
	Select/change indention	✓
	Use page numbers	✓
	Create outlines	
	Use tables	✓
	Use columns	
	Format envelopes/labels	
	Set/move tabs	
	Create/set margins	
Using Graphics	Insert images	✓
	Insert simple shapes	
	Import images	
	Clip Art	✓
	Move and resize	✓
	WordArt/Borders/Shading	✓
Print	Select print command	✓
	Select print options	✓

Publishing a Class Newspaper in Columns

Objective:

Students improve writing skills.

Students improve and increase word processing skills.

Resources:

Samples of newspapers

Example on the CD-ROM (233news2.doc)

Procedure:

1. Students should follow the first thirteen steps of the previous activity.

2. After they insert their banner, click **FORMAT** on the menu bar.

3. Choose *Columns*. Students could also click the **Columns** button on the **Standard** toolbar, but it does not give them as many options.

4. Students should choose the number of columns they want to use.

5. Students should also set the column width and change the spacing between columns or leave it at the default setting.

6. To the right of **Number of Columns** is the **Line between** box. Students could check this box to draw a line between the columns.

7. It is very important to click the **Apply to:** drop down box, and choose **This point forward**. They would have a really strange looking banner otherwise.

8. Later, if they want to change the format, for example, to have one section in two columns instead of three, students should click **FORMAT** again and change it. Be sure to choose **This point forward**, and it will not change what they have already done.

Publishing a Class Newspaper in Columns *(cont.)*

9. Students should change the tabs to make smaller paragraph indentations.

10. Students should use a different font or use bold type on the first word of an article.

11. Students should use full justification to make the edges of their columns straight.

   a. Click the **Justify** icon on the **Formatting** toolbar before they begin typing.

Or

   b. Highlight the text to align, and then click the **Justify** button on the **Formatting** toolbar.

12. This format is a little more difficult and a little more limiting in some ways because the columns overflow one into the other. Students cannot jump from one column to another to position articles, so layout and editing are both more difficult. However, this same feature can sometimes make the process easier. Because the columns flow into one another, students are not restricted by the size of the cell in a table. If one article is longer than the length of the page, it will just continue at the top of the next column. It is good to know several methods of doing things. Experiment with both methods and decide which best fits the students' needs.

13. Students should save often.

14. Students should print.

Word Processing Skills

Skill Area	Specific Skill	✓
Access a file	Open a file	✓
	Create a file	✓
	Save a file	✓
Enter text	Insert text using word wrap and return appropriately	✓
	Use shift key for capital letters	✓
Moving through a document	Use arrow keys/mouse to move cursor in document	✓
	Scroll through document	✓
Edit text	Delete text	
	Cut/copy/paste text	✓
	Search/replace text	
	Move text	
	Insert text	✓
	Select text	✓
	Spell check	✓
Manipulate format	Select/change font or font size	✓
	Select/change justification	✓
	Select/change spacing	
	Select/change indention	✓
	Use page numbers	✓
	Create outlines	
	Use tables	
	Use columns	✓
	Format envelopes/labels	
	Set/move tabs	✓
	Create/set margins	✓
Using Graphics	Insert images	✓
	Insert simple shapes	
	Import images	
	Clip Art	✓
	Move and resize	✓
	WordArt/Borders/Shading	✓
Print	Select print command	✓
	Select print options	✓

Classifying Minerals

Objective:

Students learn more about classification methods.

Students gain skill in the use of tables in *Microsoft Word*.

Resources:

Several samples of different minerals

Classification charts

Example on the CD-ROM (236class.doc)

Procedure:

1. Teachers should introduce the unit on minerals.
2. Discuss with students the characteristics of minerals and the tests available.
   a. Mohs hardness scale
   b. specific gravity test
   c. methods to test for and identify cleavage and fracture
3. Create a template for your students by opening a new blank document in *Microsoft Word*.
4. Title the page.
5. Click where you want your table to begin.
6. Click **TABLE** on the menu bar.
7. Click **Insert Table**.
8. Choose the number of columns for the number of characteristics students are going to examine.
9. Choose the same number of rows for which students have samples. You can also choose the number of rows that will easily fit on the page and still allow room to enter data.
10. Enter the names of the samples in the first cell of each row in bold type.

Classifying Minerals *(cont.)*

11. Enter the characteristic you are testing in the top cell of each column in bold type.

    a. color

    b. luster

    c. transparency (or diaphaneity)

    d. crystal systems

    e. crystal habits

    f. twinning

    g. cleavage

    h. fracture

    i. hardness

    j. streak

    k. specific gravity

12. Save the chart to a disk as your template.

13. Print enough so that each student or group will have one on which to record their data as they do the experiments.

14. After the experiments are done and the data is recorded, the students should open the file and type the results into the cells.

15. Students should save using a different name from your template.

16. Students should print the finished charts and include them in their journals.

Word Processing Skills

Skill Area	Specific Skill	✓
Access a file	Open a file	✓
	Create a file	✓
	Save a file	✓
Enter text	Insert text using word wrap and return appropriately	✓
	Use shift key for capital letters	✓
Moving through a document	Use arrow keys/mouse to move cursor in document	✓
	Scroll through document	✓
Edit text	Delete text	
	Cut/copy/paste text	
	Search/replace text	
	Move text	
	Insert text	
	Select text	
	Spell check	
Manipulate format	Select/change font or font size	
	Select/change justification	
	Select/change spacing	
	Select/change indention	
	Use page numbers	
	Create outlines	
	Use tables	✓
	Use columns	
	Format envelopes/labels	
	Set/move tabs	
	Create/set margins	
Using Graphics	Insert images	
	Insert simple shapes	
	Import images	
	Clip Art	
	Move and resize	
	WordArt/Borders/Shading	
Print	Select print command	✓
	Select print options	✓

Writing Directions

Objective:

Students effectively communicate step-by-step instructions.

Students use features of *Microsoft Word*, including creating numbered lists.

Resources:

Student disks for saving documents

List of procedures

Procedure:

1. Discuss with the class the importance of clear, concise written directions.

2. Allow students to choose from a list of ideas you created or create their own ideas.

3. Students should enter the step-by-step directions using the numbered list feature of *Microsoft Word*.

   a. Click **FORMAT** on the menu bar.

   b. Select *Bullets and Numbering*.

   c. Click the **Numbered** tab.

   d. Students should choose the type of numbering they want to use or click **Customize** to change the font, size, style, position, number to start with, and other choices.

   e. Enter the lists.

4. If students forget and start the list before formatting for a numbered list, they should highlight the list and then format. The numbers will appear after each time that they press **Enter** or **Return**.

Writing Directions *(cont.)*

5. If students forget a step and want to insert it, they should simply click at the end of the step preceding where they want to enter the new step and press **Enter** or **Return**. *Microsoft Word* will adjust the numbers accordingly.

6. Likewise, if students decide that two steps should be combined, they should place the cursor at the beginning of the second step and press the **Delete** key until the two are combined.

7. Students should check spelling and edit the document.

8. They should save the document to disk.

9. Students should print their documents and have another student try to do the steps listed to complete the task.

Word Processing Skills

Skill Area	Specific Skill	✓
Access a file	Open a file	
	Create a file	✓
	Save a file	✓
Enter text	Insert text using word wrap and return appropriately	✓
	Use shift key for capital letters	✓
Moving through a document	Use arrow keys/mouse to move cursor in document	✓
	Scroll through document	
Edit text	Delete text	✓
	Cut/copy/paste text	
	Search/replace text	
	Move text	
	Insert text	
	Select text	
	Spell check	✓
Manipulate format	Select/change font or font size	✓
	Select/change justification	
	Select/change spacing	
	Select/change indention	
	Use page numbers	
	Create outlines	
	Use tables	
	Use columns	
	Format envelopes/labels	
	Set/move tabs	
	Create/set margins	
Using Graphics	Insert images	
	Insert simple shapes	
	Import images	
	Clip Art	
	Move and resize	
	WordArt/Borders/Shading	
Print	Select print command	✓
	Select print options	✓

Fractured Fairytales

Objective:

Students gain skill in manipulating text in a *Microsoft Word* document.

Resources:

One saved document containing the fractured quotes for each student

Procedure:

1. Teachers should type quotes from familiar fairytales, but divide each quote into two parts and scramble the parts.

   a. Little Red Riding Hood said, "I am bruised all over from that bed."

   b. The giant said, "Grandmother, what big eyes you have!"

   c. The princess said, "Not by the hair of my chinny chin chin."

   d. The fairy godmother said, "Fe, Fi, Fo, Fum. I smell the blood of an Englishman."

   e. The little pig said, "Someone's been sleeping in my bed."

   f. Papa Bear said, "You must be home by midnight."

2. Students should select and move the text back to its proper place.

   a. To select the text, click and hold down the mouse button, then drag the cursor over the text until it is highlighted.

   b. Place the pointer anywhere on the selected text. Click and hold the mouse button (Macintosh) or left mouse button (Windows) as you drag the selected text to the new location. The pointer changes into a little shadowed box to show that you are moving text.

Fractured Fairytales *(cont.)*

   c. A shadowed vertical mark (like the insertion cursor, only not blinking) shows students the insertion point.

   d. When the mark is where the text is to be moved, release the mouse button to drop the text into place.

   e. Students should be sure to click in the white area to deselect the text. If they press any key with the text still highlighted, it will disappear.

   f. This is called the drag and drop method of moving text.

3. Another method to move text is the Cut and Paste method.

   a. Highlight the text.

   b. Click **EDIT** on the menu bar.

   c. Select *Cut* from the drop down menu.

   d. The selected text will disappear. It is not gone. It is in a special place called the clipboard.

   e. Position the mouse pointer in the new location for the text and click.

   f. Select **EDIT** on the menu bar.

   g. Click *Paste* from the drop down menu.

   h. Students could also select the text, then click the **Cut** button on the **Standard** toolbar (it looks like scissors). Then place the pointer at the new location, click to position the cursor, and click the **Paste** button (it looks like a clipboard).

   i. When students cut and paste, the text stays in the clipboard until it is replaced with something else. This is helpful if the same information needs to be pasted several different places in the same document.

Fractured Fairytales *(cont.)*

3. This activity can be modified for older children and different subject matters.

   a. Pablo Picasso painted *White Flower.*

   b. Frida Kahlo painted *The Artist's Father.*

   c. Vincent van Gogh painted *Les amoreaux.*

   d. Paul Cezanne painted *The Wounded Deer.*

   e. Mary Cassatt painted *The Seine with the Pont de la Grande Jette.*

   f. Georgia O'Keeffe painted *Mother About to Wash Her Sleepy Child.*

4. Students should print their corrected lists.

Word Processing Skills

Skill Area	Specific Skill	✓
Access a file	Open a file	✓
	Create a file	
	Save a file	
Enter text	Insert text using word wrap and return appropriately	
	Use shift key for capital letters	
Moving through a document	Use arrow keys/mouse to move cursor in document	✓
	Scroll through document	✓
Edit text	Delete text	
	Cut/copy/paste text	✓
	Search/replace text	
	Move text	✓
	Insert text	
	Select text	✓
	Spell check	
Manipulate format	Select/change font or font size	
	Select/change justification	
	Select/change spacing	
	Select/change indention	
	Use page numbers	
	Create outlines	
	Use tables	
	Use columns	
	Format envelopes/labels	
	Set/move tabs	
	Create/set margins	
Using Graphics	Insert images	
	Insert simple shapes	
	Import images	
	Clip Art	
	Move and resize	
	WordArt/Borders/Shading	
Print	Select print command	✓
	Select print options	✓

Book Reports

Objective:

Students communicate ideas and demonstrate comprehension of the book they read for their book report.

Students improve skills in word processing.

Resources:

Books students have read

A disk for saving their documents

Procedure:

1. Students should create a new blank document.

2. Students should write a book report in any format that they wish, as long as they include the following:
   a. title
   b. author
   c. number of pages
   d. genre
   e. four major ideas
   f. an illustration
   g. opinion of the book
   h. ten questions that can be answered by reading the book— five that are easy to answer from reading the book and five that require interpretation, judgement, or expansion of ideas.

3. Encourage students to be creative in their presentation as well as accurate and thorough in interpreting their book.

4. Students should save to disk and print.

Word Processing Skills

Skill Area	Specific Skill	✓
Access a file	Open a file	
	Create a file	✓
	Save a file	✓
Enter text	Insert text using word wrap and return appropriately	✓
	Use shift key for capital letters	✓
Moving through a document	Use arrow keys/mouse to move cursor in document	✓
	Scroll through document	✓
Edit text	Delete text	
	Cut/copy/paste text	
	Search/replace text	
	Move text	
	Insert text	
	Select text	
	Spell check	✓
Manipulate format	Select/change font or font size	✓
	Select/change justification	
	Select/change spacing	
	Select/change indention	
	Use page numbers	
	Create outlines	
	Use tables	
	Use columns	
	Format envelopes/labels	
	Set/move tabs	
	Create/set margins	
Using Graphics	Insert images	✓
	Insert simple shapes	
	Import images	
	Clip Art	
	Move and resize	✓
	WordArt/Borders/Shading	
Print	Select print command	✓
	Select print options	✓

Book Jacket Research Note Sheet

Objective:

Students learn different uses of word processing.

Resources:

A disk for saving documents

Example on the CD-ROM (248bookj.doc)

Procedure:

1. Students should create a new blank document.
2. They should change the left and right margins to 0.75" and the top margin to .5".
    a. Click **FILE** on the menu bar.
    b. Click *Page Setup* from the drop down menu.
    c. Click the **Margins** tab and change the settings.
3. Click **FORMAT** on the menu bar.
4. Click *Columns* from the drop down menu.
5. Choose three columns.
6. Click the **Equal Column Widths** box to remove the check mark.
7. Make column one 3" wide with a 0.5" space.
8. Make column two 2.75" wide with a .25" space.
9. Make column three 0.5" wide.
10. At the top of column one, in bold print, students should type *(Please return to:)*.
11. On the next three or four lines students should enter their name, address, and phone number, or name, teacher's name, and classroom.
12. Press **Enter** or **Return** until the insertion point is at the top of the second column.
13. In bold, students should type *(Notes)*.

Book Jacket Research Note Sheet *(cont.)*

14. Depending on how large the student's handwriting is, they may want to change to double-spacing at this point to make the lines farther apart.

    a. Click **FORMAT** on the menu bar.

    b. Click *Paragraph* from the drop down menu.

    c. Click the **Indents and Spacing** tab.

    d. Change the spacing to double and click **OK**.

15. Click **FORMAT** on the menu bar.

16. Select *Tabs* from the drop down menu.

17. Type *(2.7")* in the **Tab stop position** window and click **Set**.

18. Choose a solid line leader #4.

19. Make sure the alignment is set on **Left**.

20. Click the **OK** button.

21. Press **Enter** or **Return**.

22. Press **Tab** then **Enter** or **Return** repeatedly until the cursor is at the top of column 3.

23. On the top line of column 3, in bold students should type *(Page)*.

24. Click **FORMAT** on the menu bar.

25. Click *Tabs* from the drop down menu.

26. Type (0.5" in the **Tab stop position** window and click **Set**.

27. Choose Leader **#4**, the solid line leader.

28. Make sure the alignment is set on **Left**.

29. Click **OK**.

30. Press **Enter** or **Return**.

31. Press **Tab**, then **Enter** or **Return** repeatedly to the bottom of the page.

Book Jacket Research Note Sheet *(cont.)*

32. Students should save to disk and print.

33. Fold the sheet in half lengthwise and trim the bottom to match the height of the book.

34. Use tape at the top and the bottom to hold the jacket in place.

35. Students should print out several so that they can use them to record references for research papers. Students should write the name of the book and all other pertinent information on the **Please return to:** side. Then they should save the book jackets and have well-organized notes for their term paper.

Word Processing Skills

Skill Area	Specific Skill	✓
Access a file	Open a file	
	Create a file	✓
	Save a file	✓
Enter text	Insert text using word wrap and return appropriately	✓
	Use shift key for capital letters	✓
Moving through a document	Use arrow keys/mouse to move cursor in document	
	Scroll through document	
Edit text	Delete text	
	Cut/copy/paste text	
	Search/replace text	
	Move text	
	Insert text	
	Select text	
	Spell check	
Manipulate format	Select/change font or font size	✓
	Select/change justification	
	Select/change spacing	✓
	Select/change indention	
	Use page numbers	
	Create outlines	
	Use tables	
	Use columns	✓
	Format envelopes/labels	
	Set/move tabs	✓
	Create/set margins	✓
Using Graphics	Insert images	
	Insert simple shapes	
	Import images	
	Clip Art	
	Move and resize	
	WordArt/Borders/Shading	
Print	Select print command	✓
	Select print options	✓

History Report Outline

Objective:

Students develop outlines to organize information.
Students use the Outline feature of *Microsoft Word*.

Resources:

Notes from research
Student disk for saving document

Procedure:

1. Discuss thesis sentences with the students.

2. Students should create a new blank document.

3. Students should enter their thesis sentence at the beginning of the document.

4. Press **Enter** or **Return** several times to skip lines.

5. Click **VIEW** on the menu bar.

6. Click *Outline* from the drop down menu.

7. Click **FORMAT** on the menu bar

8. Click *Bullets and Numbering* from the drop down menu.

9. Click the Outline Numbered tab, and then click the view that contains Roman numeral I and the letter A. Click **OK**.

10. Students should make a list of the major points they wish to include in their report, pressing Enter or Return after each major point. They should now have the beginnings of a working outline with several Roman numerals.

History Report Outline *(cont.)*

11. Students should be ready to begin entering supporting data into their outlines. Set the cursor at the end of the first (or any other) major point, press **Enter** or **Return**.

12. On the **Outline** toolbar, press the **Right-pointing Arrow**. This will demote the line to a capital A. Students should enter their supporting data.

13. At any time, a point may be promoted a level or demoted a level by clicking the **Right** or **Left Arrows** on the **Outline** toolbar (the cursor can be anywhere within that point).

14. Outline items can also be moved around in the document by using the **Up** and **Down Arrows** on the **Outline** toolbar.

15. Students should edit, arrange, and rearrange the outline to the student's and the teacher's satisfaction; then a well-organized paper can be written.

16. Students should have the outline window open while they are writing their papers. They should then switch back and forth to refer to or change items in the outline.

17. Students should save the document to the disk.

Word Processing Skills

Skill Area	Specific Skill	✓
Access a file	Open a file	
	Create a file	✓
	Save a file	✓
Enter text	Insert text using word wrap and return appropriately	✓
	Use shift key for capital letters	✓
Moving through a document	Use arrow keys/mouse to move cursor in document	✓
	Scroll through document	✓
Edit text	Delete text	
	Cut/copy/paste text	
	Search/replace text	
	Move text	
	Insert text	
	Select text	
	Spell check	✓
Manipulate format	Select/change font or font size	
	Select/change justification	
	Select/change spacing	
	Select/change indention	
	Use page numbers	
	Create outlines	✓
	Use tables	
	Use columns	
	Format envelopes/labels	
	Set/move tabs	
	Create/set margins	
Using Graphics	Insert images	
	Insert simple shapes	
	Import images	
	Clip Art	
	Move and resize	
	WordArt/Borders/Shading	
Print	Select print command	✓
	Select print options	✓

Reading Log

Objective:

Students construct a reading log form to be used for independent reading.

Students develop and improve skills in moving and setting tab stops and using tab leaders in *Microsoft Word*.

Resources:

List of items to be included on the reading log form

Student disk to save document

Example on the CD-ROM (255log1.doc)

Procedure:

1. Students should create a new blank document.
2. Press **Ctrl + 2** (Windows) or ⌘ **+ 2** (Macintosh) to double-space the document.
3. Click **VIEW** on the menu bar.
4. Click *Headers and Footers*.

   Click inside the **Header** box and enter *(Name:)*.
6. Close the **Header and Footer** toolbar.
7. At the top of the page, use the **Center Alignment** button on the **Formatting** toolbar to center the title, *(Reading Log)*, and press **Enter** or **Return**.
8. Students should put a small piece of clip art before and/or after the title. In the example on the CD-ROM, an owl from the academic section of the clip art gallery was used and the picture was formatted to wrap tightly on both sides.
   a. With the clip art selected, go to **FORMAT** on the menu bar, then choose *Picture* and the **Wrapping** tab. Select the type of word wrap and click **OK**.
9. Click **FORMAT** on the menu bar.
10. Click *Columns*.

Reading Log *(cont.)*

11. Choose 5 columns with widths of 0.6" for columns 1, 3, 4 and 5 and 2" for column 2. Enter 0.4" spacing on each.
12. Click the **Apply to:** box and choose **This point forward**.
13. Click **FORMAT** on the menu bar.
14. Click *Tabs* from the drop down menu.
15. Click **Clear all**.
16. Click in the **Tab stop position** box and enter *(0.6")*.
17. Click the circle next to **#4**, the solid line leader.
18. Click **Set** and **OK**.
19. Enter the word *(Date)* on the top line of the first column and press **Enter** or **Return**.
20. Press the **Tab** key and then **Enter** or **Return** for each line in the first column.
21. When the cursor is at the top of the second column, go again to *Tabs* on the **FORMAT** menu.
22. This time click **Clear all** and then enter *(2")* in the **Tab stop position** box.
23. Set the solid line leader.
24. Click **Set** and **OK**.
25. Enter the word *(Book Title)* on the top line of the second column and press **Enter** or **Return.**
26. Press the **Tab** key and then **Enter** or **Return** for each line in the second column.
27. For columns 3, 4, and 5 set the tab for *(0.6")* and set the leader for a solid line. Type the headings *(Pages)*, *(Time)*, and *(Initials)* on each column respectively.
28. Press **Tab** and **Enter** or **Return** to put lines in the columns. Go back to the top of the columns. Highlight and center each column heading.
29. Students should save the document to their disks and print as needed.

Word Processing Skills

Skill Area	Specific Skill	✓
Access a file	Open a file	
	Create a file	✓
	Save a file	✓
Enter text	Insert text using word wrap and return appropriately	✓
	Use shift key for capital letters	✓
Moving through a document	Use arrow keys/mouse to move cursor in document	✓
	Scroll through document	✓
Edit text	Delete text	
	Cut/copy/paste text	
	Search/replace text	
	Move text	
	Insert text	
	Select text	
	Spell check	
Manipulate format	Select/change font or font size	✓
	Select/change justification	
	Select/change spacing	✓
	Select/change indention	
	Use page numbers	
	Create outlines	
	Use tables	
	Use columns	✓
	Format envelopes/labels	
	Set/move tabs	✓
	Create/set margins	
Using Graphics	Insert images	✓
	Insert simple shapes	
	Import images	
	Clip Art	✓
	Move and resize	✓
	WordArt/Borders/Shading	
Print	Select print command	✓
	Select print options	✓

Another Reading Log

Objective:

Students construct a reading log form to be used for independent reading.

Students develop and improve skills in creating and editing documents containing tables in *Microsoft Word*.

Resources:

List of items to include on the reading log form

Student disk to save document

Example on the CD-ROM (258log2.doc)

Procedure:

1. Students should create a new blank document.
2. Press **Ctrl + 2** (Windows) or ⌘ **+ 2** (Macintosh) to double-space the document.
3. Click **VIEW** on the menu bar.
4. Click *Headers and Footers*.
5. Click inside the **Header** box and enter *(Name:)*.
6. Close the **Header and Footer** toolbar.
7. Change the font size to 20. This will make the cells larger.
8. Click **TABLE** on the menu bar.
9. Click *Insert Table* and choose 5 columns and 25 rows.
10. Click the arrow to the left of row 1. This will highlight the row.
11. Click **TABLE** on the menu bar and select *Cell Height and Width*.

Another Reading Log *(cont.)*

12. When the dialog box appears, select the **Row** tab. A selection box will indicate **Height of row 1**. In the box after the word **At:**, enter *(50 pt)*. This will make the first row wider than the rest.

13. If the Tables and Borders toolbar is not visible, click **VIEW**, then *Toolbars*, then *Tables and Borders*.

14. Click the **Eraser** and drag it over the cell divisions in row 1, leaving just one large undivided row.

15. Click inside row 1, and then click the **Center Alignment** button on the **Formatting** toolbar and the **Vertical Alignment** button on the **Tables and Borders** toolbar.

16. Insert clip art, resize it, space several times, and enter *(Reading Log)*. Space the same number of times and insert clip art again.

17. Students may have trouble getting their clip art to stay where they want it.

    a. Click the picture to select it.

    b. Click *Picture* (or Object) on the **FORMAT** menu.

    c. Click the **Position** tab.

    d. Make sure that the box next to **Float over text** is NOT checked.

18. Again click outside of the table, to the left of row 2. This will highlight the row. Click the **Center Alignment** button on the **Formatting** toolbar.

19. Click inside the cells and enter the headings, *(Date)*, *(Book Title)*, *(Pages)*, *(Time)*, and *(Initials)*.

20. Students should save the document and print as needed.

Word Processing Skills

Skill Area	Specific Skill	✓
Access a file	Open a file	
	Create a file	✓
	Save a file	✓
Enter text	Insert text using word wrap and return appropriately	✓
	Use shift key for capital letters	✓
Moving through a document	Use arrow keys/mouse to move cursor in document	✓
	Scroll through document	
Edit text	Delete text	
	Cut/copy/paste text	
	Search/replace text	
	Move text	
	Insert text	
	Select text	✓
	Spell check	·
Manipulate format	Select/change font or font size	✓
	Select/change justification	
	Select/change spacing	
	Select/change indention	
	Use page numbers	
	Create outlines	
	Use tables	✓
	Use columns	
	Format envelopes/labels	
	Set/move tabs	
	Create/set margins	
Using Graphics	Insert images	✓
	Insert simple shapes	
	Import images	
	Clip Art	✓
	Move and resize	✓
	WordArt/Borders/Shading	
Print	Select print command	✓
	Select print options	✓

Great American Mail Race— Part One

The Great American Mail Race is a nation-wide project in which school-age children write letters telling other school children about their school and community. The children choose cities and schools from a lengthy list of participating schools. They each write two letters initially, and then answer any letters that other children send to them. They love to have special stationary that is different from "just plain notebook paper," and adding the school mascot to these mailers makes them very popular.

The Great American Mail Race has a Web site on the Internet. Access this site by going to Yahoo.com and typing in *(Great American Mail Race)* or **http://idt.net/~urbanch/courtlandt/mailrace.html**

Objective:

Students enrich their knowledge of geography, social studies, and the art of communication.

Students increase their skill with the word processor.

Resources:

U.S. Maps, atlases, encyclopedias, almanacs, and access to the Internet

Medium or lightweight cardstock

Colored stickers or cellophane tape

Student disks to save documents

Examples on the CD-ROM (261mail1.doc and 261mail2.doc)

Procedure:

1. Students should create a new blank document.

Great American Mail Race— Part One *(cont.)*

2. Click **TABLE** on the menu bar.

3. Click *Insert Table* from the drop down menu.

4. Set the table for 1 column and 27 rows and click **OK**.

5. Click just above the table to select it all.

6. On the **TABLE** menu, click *Cell Height and Width*.

7. Click the **Row** tab and in the box after the word **At:**, enter *(22)* and click **OK**.

8. If the Tables and Borders toolbar is not visible, go to **VIEW**, then *Toolbars*, then *Tables and Borders*.

9. Click the pencil and draw a vertical line about 20 characters from the right edge of the table and down 4 rows. This will be an area for students to type in a return address.

10. Students should click inside the area that they have just created and enter their return address.

11. This part is a little tricky.

   a. Highlight just the return address area.

   b. Click the down arrow by the **Border** button just a bit to the left of the **Font Color** button on the Formatting toolbar.

   c. Click the **Left Border** button.

   d. This should make the line to the left of the return address invisible.

Great American Mail Race— Part One *(cont.)*

12. Students should choose a piece of artwork for their watermark.

13. On the **VIEW** menu, click *Header and Footer*.

14. Insert the graphic.
    a. Click **INSERT** on the menu bar.
    b. Click *Picture* on the drop down menu.
    c. Students should click either *ClipArt* or *From file*, depending on what kind of artwork they have chosen.

15. Students should resize the graphic and move it where they want it placed.

16. Select the graphic and then click **FORMAT** on the menu bar.

17. Click *Picture* (or Object).

18. On the **Picture** tab, under **Image Control**, click in the **Color** box and choose **Watermark**.

    a. Students should adjust the brightness and contrast if they want it more or less visible.

19. On the **Wrapping** tab, select **None** and click **OK**.

20. On the **Header and Footer** toolbar, click **Close**.

21. Students should save the document to disk.

22. Students should print on lightweight cardstock. Paper will work, but cards arrive at their destination in better shape when heavier paper is used.

Great American Mail Race— Part Two

Procedure:

For the outside of the mailer:

1. Students should create a new blank document.
2. Click **INSERT** on the menu bar.
3. Click *Text Box*.
4. Scroll down about $1/2$" below the halfway point of the page, about the 5" mark on the ruler.
5. Click and drag the mouse from the left margin to the right margin to the bottom margin.
6. Change to size 10 font.
7. In the top left corner of the text box, students should type their return address.
8. Click **INSERT** on the menu bar and click *Text Box*.
9. Place the new text box a little toward the bottom and right of center inside the larger text box, making a box for the mailing address.
10. Students should type four lines inside the smaller text box using the **Underline** tool and double-spacing.
11. Click outside the smaller text box, but make sure the cursor is still inside the larger one.
12. Insert a graphic, resize it, and place it to the left of the address box.
13. Print Part Two on the back of Part One.
14. Students should write their letter, fold top to bottom, secure with a sticker, address, stamp, and mail.

Great American Mail Race *(cont.)*

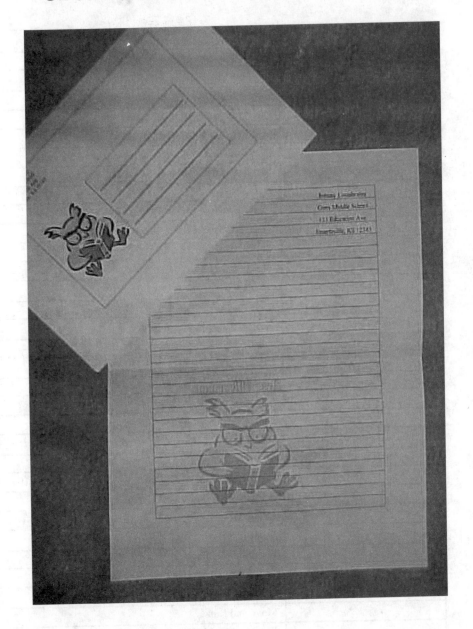

Word Processing Skills

Skill Area	Specific Skill	✓
Access a file	Open a file	
	Create a file	✓
	Save a file	✓
Enter text	Insert text using word wrap and return appropriately	✓
	Use shift key for capital letters	✓
Moving through a document	Use arrow keys/mouse to move cursor in document	✓
	Scroll through document	✓
Edit text	Delete text	
	Cut/copy/paste text	
	Search/replace text	
	Move text	
	Insert text	
	Select text	✓
	Spell check	
Manipulate format	Select/change font or font size	✓
	Select/change justification	
	Select/change spacing	✓
	Select/change indention	
	Use page numbers	
	Create outlines	
	Use tables	✓
	Use columns	
	Format envelopes/labels	
	Set/move tabs	
	Create/set margins	
Using Graphics	Insert images	✓
	Insert simple shapes	
	Import images	
	Clip Art	✓
	Move and resize	✓
	WordArt/Borders/Shading	✓
Print	Select print command	✓
	Select print options	✓

The Human Body Corporation

This lesson plan is not one I designed. I have used it with my students to teach letter writing and research. They love it! So with permission from Kyle Yamnitz, I am including it for you. Please visit his Web page for more lesson plans.

Elementary Education Lesson Plans:

http://www.lessonplanspage.com

Your Basic Computer Hardware Page:

http://www.lessonplanspage.com/computer/

Objective:

Students learn letter writing techniques and research skills.

Resources:

Information about the human body, its organs and systems

Student disks to save letter

Description:

As body organs, students are employees of the Human Body Corporation. Due to recent cost increases, the Human Body must fire workers. Students need to write a letter to the Human Body Corporation defending their position in the company. In their letter, they need to describe the following characteristics of their organ to the corporation and explain why they are important to the Human Body Corporation.

1. State the name of your organ and where you are located.

2. Identify the systems of the body with whom you work.

3. Describe how you work with these systems.

4. List the other organs that work with you in your system.

5. Describe your main functions as a Human Body organ.

The Human Body Corporation *(cont.)*

6. Tell the corporation how you perform these functions.

7. Tell the corporation why you are important, and why they should not fire you.

8. Explain what might happen to the Human Body Corporation if they did fire you.

9. You will read your letter to the Human Body Committee (the rest of the class). Along with your letter, you will need to have a photograph (or labeled drawing) of your organ to use as a visual aid.

Word Processing Skills

Skill Area	Specific Skill	✓
Access a file	Open a file	
	Create a file	✓
	Save a file	✓
Enter text	Insert text using word wrap and return appropriately	✓
	Use shift key for capital letters	✓
Moving through a document	Use arrow keys/mouse to move cursor in document	✓
	Scroll through document	
Edit text	Delete text	
	Cut/copy/paste text	
	Search/replace text	
	Move text	
	Insert text	
	Select text	
	Spell check	✓
Manipulate format	Select/change font or font size	
	Select/change justification	
	Select/change spacing	✓
	Select/change indention	
	Use page numbers	
	Create outlines	
	Use tables	
	Use columns	
	Format envelopes/labels	✓
	Set/move tabs	✓
	Create/set margins	
Using Graphics	Insert images	
	Insert simple shapes	
	Import images	
	Clip Art	
	Move and resize	
	WordArt/Borders/Shading	
Print	Select print command	✓
	Select print options	✓

Coupon Letter

Objective:

Students gain skill in letter writing formats.

Students learn varied applications for the word processor.

Resources:

Information for a bake sale

Student disks for saving documents

Example on the CD-ROM (270coup.doc)

Procedure:

1. Students should create a new blank document.
2. They should set the top margin for 2.5 inches.
   a. Click **FILE** on the menu bar.
   b. Click *Page Setup* on the drop down menu.
   c. Click the **Margins** tab and set the top margin.
3. Set the tabs for the return address, closing, and name, if using the modified block style.
   a. Click the small button at the far left of the horizontal ruler until it changes to the type of tab needed. In this case, it needs to be a left tab.
   b. Click at the point on the horizontal ruler where a tab stop needs to be set.
4. If students want to set precise measurements for tabs, select *Tabs* from the **FORMAT** menu.
5. Have students enter the information describing the bake sale and ask for contributions.
6. Press **Enter** until the cursor is three inches from the bottom of the page.

Coupon Letter *(cont.)*

7. Set a left tab at the right margin with a dashed line leader.
    a. Click **FORMAT** on the menu bar.
    b. Click *Tabs* on the drop down menu.
    c. Click the **Clear All** button.
    d. Enter *(6")* in the **Tab Stop Position** box.
    e. Check the little circle beside leader **#3**, the dashed line leader.
    f. Click **Set** and **OK**.
8. Press the **Tab** key. This will place a dashed line across the page.
9. Students should type *(Cut here and return the lower portion to your child's teacher)*.
10. Click **FORMAT** on the menu bar.
11. Click *Paragraph* on the drop down menu.
12. Click the **Indents and Spacing** tab, and change to double spacing.
13. Reset the tab at 6", but this time choose a solid underline leader.
14. Have students enter the parent survey information and be sure to include a signature line.
    a. *(I will furnish _____ for the bake sale.)*
    b. *(I can not participate in this activity but please keep me in mind for _____ .)*
    c. *(Signed: _____)*
15. Students should save to a disk and print.

Word Processing Skills

Skill Area	Specific Skill	✓
Access a file	Open a file	
	Create a file	✓
	Save a file	✓
Enter text	Insert text using word wrap and return appropriately	✓
	Use shift key for capital letters	✓
Moving through a document	Use arrow keys/mouse to move cursor in document	✓
	Scroll through document	✓
Edit text	Delete text	
	Cut/copy/paste text	
	Search/replace text	
	Move text	
	Insert text	
	Select text	
	Spell check	✓
Manipulate format	Select/change font or font size	
	Select/change justification	
	Select/change spacing	✓
	Select/change indention	
	Use page numbers	
	Create outlines	
	Use tables	
	Use columns	
	Format envelopes/labels	
	Set/move tabs	✓
	Create/set margins	✓
Using Graphics	Insert images	
	Insert simple shapes	
	Import images	
	Clip Art	
	Move and resize	
	WordArt/Borders/Shading	
Print	Select print command	✓
	Select print options	✓

Certificates

Microsoft, on their Web site, has provided Classroom Tools, Teacher Tools, and Student Tools for you to download. Their Web address is:

http://www.microsoft.com/education/k12/office/tools.htm

Objective:

Students make certificates using Student Tools in *Microsoft Office*.

Resources:

Templates downloaded from the Microsoft Web site

Procedure:

1. Students should open a new blank document.

2. Click the **Student Tools** tab and then *Certificate.dot*. This is a template.

3. Click the first blue area and the entire area will be highlighted. Students should type in the school name, and it will replace the words that are there.

4. Students should select the next blue area and type in a student's name.

5. Any of the items on the certificate can be modified or replaced.

6. Students should name and save the document.

7. Students should print the certificate on heavy paper.

Invitation to Open House

Objective:

Students learn to format a *Microsoft Word* document to make a brochure.

Resources:

Student disks to save document

Clip art

Information concerning dates, times, and schedule of the School Open House

Example on the CD-ROM (274open.doc)

Procedure:

1. Students should create a new blank document.
2. Click **FILE**, then on *Page Setup*.
3. Click the **Paper Size** tab and select **Landscape**.
4. Click the **Margins** tab or button and make the margins as small as the printer will allow (usually .5" for landscape).
5. Students should divide the sheet into thirds mentally. Deducting a two inch space (half inch on either side of the folds), about two and one-third inches should be left in working space for each section.
6. Estimate the size of each section of information students should put into their brochure. One way to organize the brochure would be to have a section for each subject area.
7. Make a text box for each section. Students should resize them later if they are not exactly the right size for the information.
   a. Click **INSERT** on the menu bar.
   b. Click *Text box* from the drop down menu.

Invitation to Open House *(cont.)*

    c. Press and hold the mouse button while dragging diagonally down until the text box is the desired size.

    d. Click inside the text box to begin entering data or graphics.

8. Students should create two documents. One will be the inside of their brochure. The other will be the outside. The front of the brochure will be the far right section of the outside.

9. Save both documents to disk.

10. Print one side. Put the paper back into the printer, paying attention to the direction it prints and on which side of the sheet it prints.

11. Print the other side.

12. Fold carefully.

Note: There is also a brochure template in the Student Tools download mentioned in the previous activity.

Bookmarks

Objective:

Students explore another use for text boxes and tables.

Resources:

Student disks for saving documents

Clip art

Fancy edge-cutting scissors

Examples on the CD-ROM (276bkmk1.doc, 276bkmk2.doc)

Procedure:

1. Students should create a new blank document.

2. They should insert text boxes approximately 1.5 inches wide and leaving at least an inch between.

3. Six inches long is a good size for bookmarks, but different students have different preferences.

4. The students should save their document at this point, so they will have blank templates to decorate later.

5. Students should personalize and decorate their bookmarks with unique fonts, graphics, quotes, etc.

6. Print the document.

7. Students should cut around the bookmarks with pinking shears or the fancy scissors available at discount stores, fabric stores, and hobby shops.

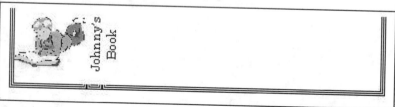

Class Memory Book—Part One

Objective:

Students create a classroom memory book by entering their own autobiographical information into a document.

Students gain experience in copying, pasting, and inserting files.

Resources:

Digital camera, if available

Scanner, if available

Pictures of the students

Comb binder, if available

Procedure:

1. Students should discuss what makes writing interesting.
2. Have a class discussion to set up rules and guidelines for the information to be included in the class memory book. Make the guidelines positive by making it clear what is appropriate.
3. Either scan photographs or take pictures of students using a digital camera.
4. Students should create a new blank document.
5. Press **Ctrl + 2** (Windows) or ⌘ + **2** to double-space.
6. Create a Heading Style for the titles.
   a. Click the **Style** box on the **Formatting** toolbar.
   b. Click **Heading 1** from the drop down menu.
   c. Click **FORMAT** on the menu bar.
   d. Click *Style* from the drop down menu.
   e. In the **Styles** box, select **Heading 1**.

Class Memory Book—Part One

(cont.)

      f. Click the **Modify** button.

      g. Click **Format**, and then click **Font**.

      h. Change to the font style and size for the page titles and click **OK**.

7. Insert the pertinent photograph into the document.

      a. Click **INSERT** on the menu bar.

      b. Point to *Picture* on the drop down menu and select **From File**.

      c. Click in the **Look in:** box and open the file (Windows) or select the file from the dialog box (Macintosh).

8. Move and resize the photograph as desired.

      a. Click the photograph to select it.

      b. Move the pointer over the edges of the selection.

      c. If the pointer is a two-headed arrow, click and drag to resize.

      d. If the pointer is a four-headed arrow, click and drag to move.

9. Students should begin to enter autobiographical information to go with the picture.

10. Add other clip art, quotes, borders, etc. as desired.

11. Teachers should supervise to make sure only appropriate material is included.

12. Save the documents to disk.

13. Students should read each other's entries and assist with editing.

14. Save the documents again, if necessary.

Part Two—Putting It Together

1. Choose one student or a group of students to put the Class Memory Book together.

2. The students should create a new blank document.

3. They should make a title page. For example, *Class of 2006* or *Mrs. Korzenewsky's Science Class—Now and in the Future.*

4. Insert a page break.

   a. Click **INSERT** on the menu bar.

   b. Click *Break*.

   c. Click **Page Break**.

5. Type *(Table of Contents)* in a nice, large, easy-to-read font.

6. Insert another page break.

7. Place the disk containing one of the autobiographies into the disk drive.

8. Click **INSERT** on the menu bar.

9. Click *File* from the drop down menu.

10. Locate the desired file and click **Open** (Windows) or **Insert** (Macintosh).

11. Students should repeat with each student document to be included into the book.

12. Scroll up to the Table of Contents page.

13. Click **INSERT** on the menu bar.

14. Click *Index and Tables* from the drop down menu bar.

15. Click the **Table of Contents** tab and **OK**.

16. If everyone has used Heading 1 for his or her titles, the Table of Contents should be complete.

17. Students should put a footer on each page with the page number in it. They do not have to actually add the specific numbers to each page—the footer will insert the page numbers for the whole document.

Part Two—
Putting It Together *(cont.)*

17. Scroll down to the first page of the first story, skipping the Title page and the Table of Contents page.

   a. Click **VIEW** on the menu bar.

   b. Select *Header and Footer*.

   c. Scroll down and click inside the **Footer**.

   d. Click the **Center Alignment** button on the **Formatting** toolbar, the bar with the font style and font size on it. The alignment buttons have little horizontal lines on them.

   e. Click the **Insert Page Numbers** button on the **Header and Footer** toolbar. It should be in the center of the page now.

   f. Click the **Page Setup** button on the **Header and Footer** toolbar. It looks like an open book.

   g. In the dialog box, select the down triangle beside the box that says **Apply to:** and choose **From this point forward**.

18. Close the **Header and Footer** toolbar. The page numbers will now appear at the bottom of the page in the center.

19. Students should edit, save, and print one complete document for everyone in the class.

20. Bind with a comb binder if one is available or put into a three-ring binder.

Making A Story Web

Objective:

Students create a graphic representation using basic shapes and drawing tools.

Students use a story web to prepare to write stories.

Resources:

Story prompts

Student disks for saving documents

Example on the CD-ROM (281web.doc)

Procedure:

1. Teachers should review writing techniques with students.
2. Teachers should review brainstorming techniques with students.
3. Teachers should explain what a story web is, how it helps organize thoughts, and how it works.
4. Students should create a new blank document.
5. Click **VIEW** on the menu bar.
6. Select *Toolbars* and choose *Drawing* from the menu. The **Drawing** toolbar should appear on the screen.
7. In the **AutoShapes** section of the **Drawing** toolbar, click the **Oval** button. This will change the mouse pointer into a plus sign.
8. Place the pointer approximately in the center of the document page, click and hold, and drag down diagonally to make a circle in the center of the page.
9. When the circle gets to the size and shape desired, release the mouse button.
10. While the circle is selected, click, hold, and drag to reposition it if it is not in the center.

Making A Story Web *(cont.)*

11. Select the **Oval** button again. Click and drag the mouse to make a slightly smaller circle.

12. Position it above the large circle.

13. Select the smaller circle, click **EDIT** on the menu bar, and click *Copy* from the drop down menu.

14. Select **EDIT** and then *Paste*. Another circle will appear. Reposition it below the large circle.

15. Continue to select **EDIT** and *Paste* until there are eight circles positioned around the center circle.

16. Click the **Line** button in the **AutoShapes** section of the **Drawing** toolbar.

17. Again the mouse pointer will change to a plus.

18. Draw a line from the center circle to each of the smaller circles.

    a. Students should click the **Line** button and draw each of the lines, or they should draw one, then use **Copy** and **Paste** for each new line needed.

    b. It can be difficult to position the line exactly right using the (+).

    c. After the line is drawn, students should reposition and resize it just like any other drawing, by placing the mouse pointer on the little squares, clicking, and then dragging.

    d. Resize and reposition each line as needed.

19. Students should now put lines inside all of the circles so they can write in them.

    a. Click the **Line** button and draw a line across the top and outside of one of the small circles.

Making A Story Web *(cont.)*

    b. Click **EDIT** and then *Copy*.

    c. Click **EDIT** and then *Paste* about 5 times.

20. Students should hold down the **Shift** key as they select each line. This will allow them to select all of the lines together.

    a. Click the word **Draw** on the **Drawing** toolbar and select **Align** or **Distribute**.

    b. Click **Align Left**.

    c. While all of the lines are still selected, drag and position them inside one of the circles.

21. Click the mouse in a white area to deselect the lines then position the top and the bottom lines near the top and the bottom of the circle.

    a. Holding down the **Shift** key, again select all of the lines.

    b. Click **Draw** on the **Drawing** toolbar and select **Align** or **Distribute**. Click **Distribute Vertically**.

    c. Click **Draw** on the **Drawing** toolbar and click **Group**.

    d. Click **EDIT** and then *Copy*.

    e. Now you can click **EDIT** and then *Paste* to add lines inside each of the circles.

22. Students should save the document to disk and print as needed.

23. Students should choose a main idea for their story.

24. They should write that idea in the center circle.

25. They should brainstorm with their group to develop more ideas branching off from the main idea and write those in the smaller circles.

26. They should number each of the smaller circles and develop webs for each of those.

27. When students have developed their webs and arranged them just the way they want them, they should make an outline. This can make writing their story easier.

Making A Story Web *(cont.)*

The Story Web can also be a very useful tool for students to use to develop characters.

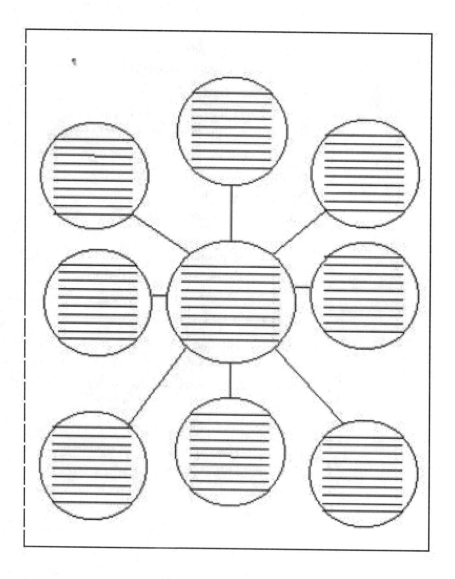

Word Processing Skills

Skill Area	Specific Skill	✓
Access a file	Open a file	✓
	Create a file	✓
	Save a file	✓
Enter text	Insert text using word wrap and return appropriately	✓
	Use shift key for capital letters	✓
Moving through a document	Use arrow keys/mouse to move cursor in document	✓
	Scroll through document	✓
Edit text	Delete text	
	Cut/copy/paste text	✓
	Search/replace text	
	Move text	
	Insert text	✓
	Select text	✓
	Spell check	✓
Manipulate format	Select/change font or font size	✓
	Select/change justification	
	Select/change spacing	✓
	Select/change indention	
	Use page numbers	✓
	Create outlines	✓
	Use tables	
	Use columns	
	Format envelopes/labels	
	Set/move tabs	
	Create/set margins	
Using Graphics	Insert images	✓
	Insert simple shapes	✓
	Import images	
	Clip Art	
	Move and resize	✓
	WordArt/Borders/Shading	
Print	Select print command	✓
	Select print options	✓

Original Poetry

This is a culminating activity to a unit on poetry. During the unit, the students write original poetry using rhyme, free verse, blank verse, different examples of meter, etc.

Objective:

Students decide which of their work is the best for publication. Students format the documents to best display their work.

Resources:

Students' original poetry

Clip art or students' original art

Procedure:

1. Students should choose several of their best poems. Explain that even professional writers do not always publish everything they write. Discuss the reasons why.

2. Discuss the pieces chosen and the reasons for choosing those pieces.

3. Each student should decide how best to display each of his/her poems.

4. Students should pick the shading for their document.

   a. Click ***Borders and Shading*** on the **FORMAT** menu.
   b. Click the **Shading** tab.
   c. Choose the pattern style and color.
   d. Choose the fill color and click **OK**.

Original Poetry *(cont.)*

5. Students should pick the borders for their document.

   a. Click ***Borders and Shading*** on the **FORMAT** menu.

   b. Click the **Page Border** tab

   c. Select the page border options they want and click **OK**. Students should check out the **Art:** menu button.

6. Students should pick the WordArt for their document.

   a. Click **INSERT** on the menu bar.

   b. Place the mouse pointer over the word ***Picture***.

   c. Select ***WordArt***.

   d. Choose the options that apply and click **OK**.

7. Students should pick the Illustrations for their document.

   a. Draw or scan pictures from a drawing program that does original computer drawings. Scan photographs or use a digital camera to take photographs. Students should save their file.

   b. Click **INSERT** on the menu bar.

   c. Place your mouse pointer over the word ***Picture***.

   d. Select ***From File***.

   e. Locate the saved file and click **Open** or **Insert**.

   f. Resize and move the picture to the desired position.

8. Students should pick a Watermark for their document.

   a. Choose a piece of artwork for the watermark.

   b. On the **VIEW** menu, click ***Header and Footer***.

   c. Insert the graphic.

   d. Resize the graphic and move it to the desired position.

   e. Select the graphic and then click **FORMAT** on the menu bar.

Original Poetry *(cont.)*

    f. Click *Picture* or *Object*.

    g. On the **Picture** tab, under **Image Control**, click in the **Color** box and choose **Watermark**.

    h. Students should adjust the brightness and contrast if they want it more or less visible.

    i. On the **Header and Footer** toolbar, click **Close**.

9. Students could also pick an interesting form for their document. They could arrange their words on the page to portray an idea or picture.

10. Students could pick different fonts and more for their document.

11. The students should use all of their word processing skills to achieve the desired effects.

Glossary

3-D—Three-dimensional effects used in graphics.

Alignment—Formatting tool used to left, right, center, or full justify text.

Animation—Movement used with text and graphics to enhance appearance.

AutoSum—Addition of a column of numbers in the Table feature.

Barcode—Computer generated coding used in postal delivery systems.

Block of text—Any group of contiguous words.

Bookmarks—Relative place identifiers used to provide easy access to an area of the document.

Break—Page or section breaks used to segment the document for formatting.

Bullets—Graphic symbols used in lists to identify individual items.

Cell—An area in a table where data may be entered.

Collapse—To reduce the number of levels seen in an outline.

Collate—Copies printed will be in 1, 2, 3 order.

Ctrl (**Control key**) (Windows) or ⌘ (Command key) (Macintosh)—Used in combination with other keys to broaden features available in *Microsoft Word*.

Crop—To cut off or trim part of a picture or graphic.

Customize—Features that permit the user to set preferences in functionality or appearance.

Decimal tab—Tab setting where all numbers are right aligned.

Demote—To lessen the level of importance in an outline.

Effect—A change in appearance of a font or graphic.

Even Distribution—To make all rows or columns in a table equal in size.

Expand—To show a greater number of levels in an outline.

Fill—The color or pattern used in solid areas of a shape.

Folder—A method of organizing filed documents into categories.

Font—The design style of the typeface.

Footer—An area in a document where information is entered and displayed at the bottom of every page.

Full justified—Lines of type meet both left and right margins.

Gallery—The catalog of clip art used for viewing and selecting.

Grayscale—The adjustment of color photos into shades of gray for printing and effects.

Handles—The small boxes that appear when sizing and moving graphics.

Hanging indentations—Paragraph formatting where the first line is at the left margin and subsequent lines are several spaces from the left margin.

Headers— An area in a document where information is entered and displayed at the top of every page.

HTML—Hypertext Media Language used on the Internet for developing Web pages.

Hyphenate—To break a word into two parts for line ending decisions.

I-beam—The shape of the cursor in *Microsoft Word* which represents the point where typing can begin.

Icon—A small picture that represents an action if selected.

Import—To bring in graphics or text that were not created in *Microsoft Word*.

Indentation—The start of a line that is further from the margin than the remainder of the document.

Landscape—The document is turned so that the long side of the document is the top edge of the page.

Leader dots—The small dots between a topic and the page number on a table of contents.

Match case—In Find and Replace, the requirement that the same capitalization exist in the findings as in the entry.

Maximize—To make as large as possible.

Merge—To join together data from one document with a form in a second document.

Minimize—To make as small as possible.

Nudge—To move a graphic by lines or pixels using arrow the keys.

Numeric keypad—Keys on right side of keyboard that facilitate efficient entry of numbers.

Orphan—The first line of a paragraph that ends up at the bottom of a page when the reminder of the paragraph is on the next page.

Pagination—How a document is broken into pages, whether automatically or intentionally.

Portrait—The short side of the document is the top of the page.

Preview—To look at a document prior to printing or to look at an effect prior to applying it to the document.

Promote—To make a topic of greater importance in an outline.

Properties—Settings on a printer or program that control an operation.

Redo—To re-instate an action previously cancelled.

Scroll—To move through a document or screen.

Section—A part of the document with different formatting.

Text box—A box inserted in a document that allows typing outside of the normal document format.

Typeface—The font including style effects.

Undo—To erase or delete an action.

Watermark—To make a picture transparent for use as a background.

Widow—The last line of a paragraph that ends up at the top of the next page.

Window—Something to stare out of when you're trying to think of a new project in *Microsoft Word*.

Wrap—If a sentence is not complete at the end of a line, the first letter of the next word will automatically start on the next line.

Zoom—To change the view on the screen to either a larger or smaller view, from multiple pages (10%) to huge type (500%).

Index

D

G

H

I

T

CD-ROM Filenames